ELSEWHERE

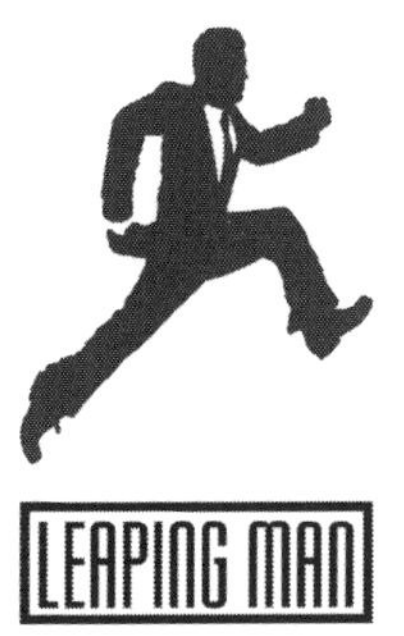

KATHERINE OKTOBER MATTHEWS

ELSEWHERE

A PERSONAL ESSAY IN WORDS & PHOTOS

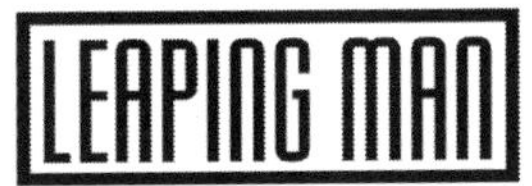

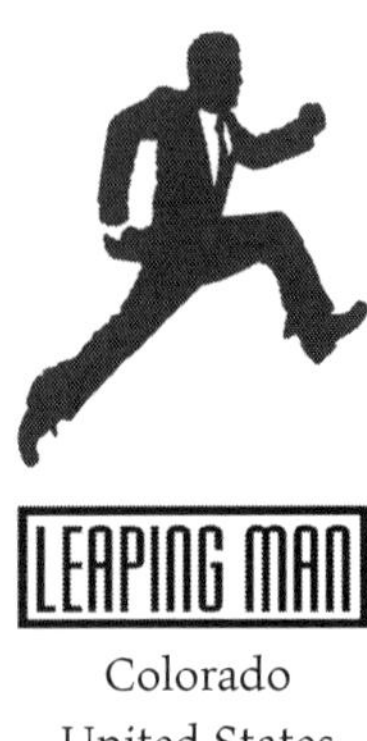

Colorado
United States

All photographs and texts
Copyright © 2025 by Katherine Oktober Matthews

ISBN: 978-0-9985922-2-0

2025
leapingman.org

Book design by Katherine Oktober Matthews

For Wayne Milstead
(1971 - 2023)
— a friend and editor of noble depths —
in gratitude for his support of this book
before it was a book

LET'S start with THIS:

It feels good to go. To be moving.

I get restless after a time, when everything starts adding up. It feels good to say a dramatic goodbye, one of those "I wish I didn't have to leave" kinds with passionate kisses and tears choked back. But it feels just as good to say "fuck this" and walk out without looking back. Some people, mostly the ones left behind, think it's the coward's way out, because you don't stick around to see things through. But moving around means two things: You're leaving one thing behind, and you're going toward something else.

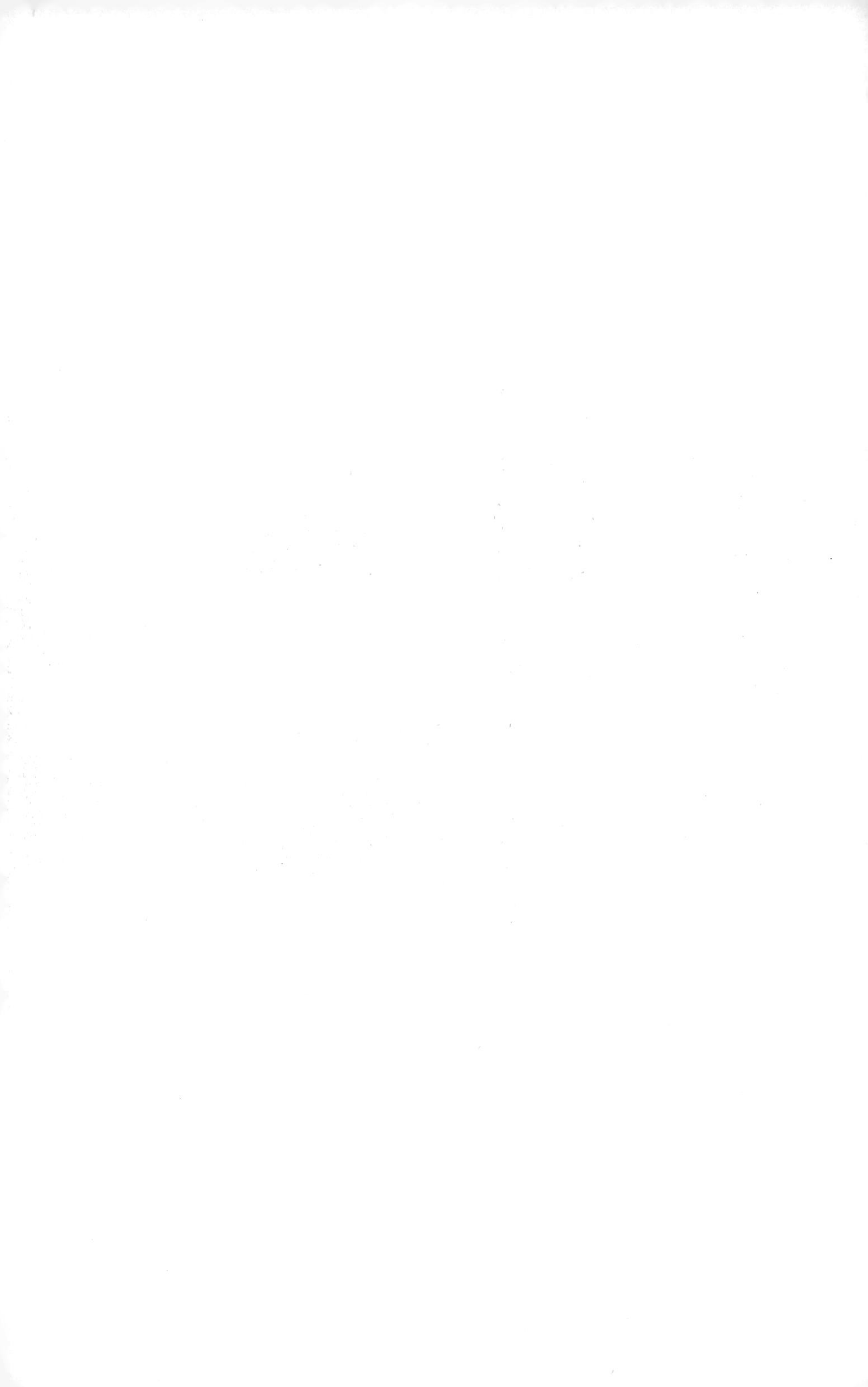

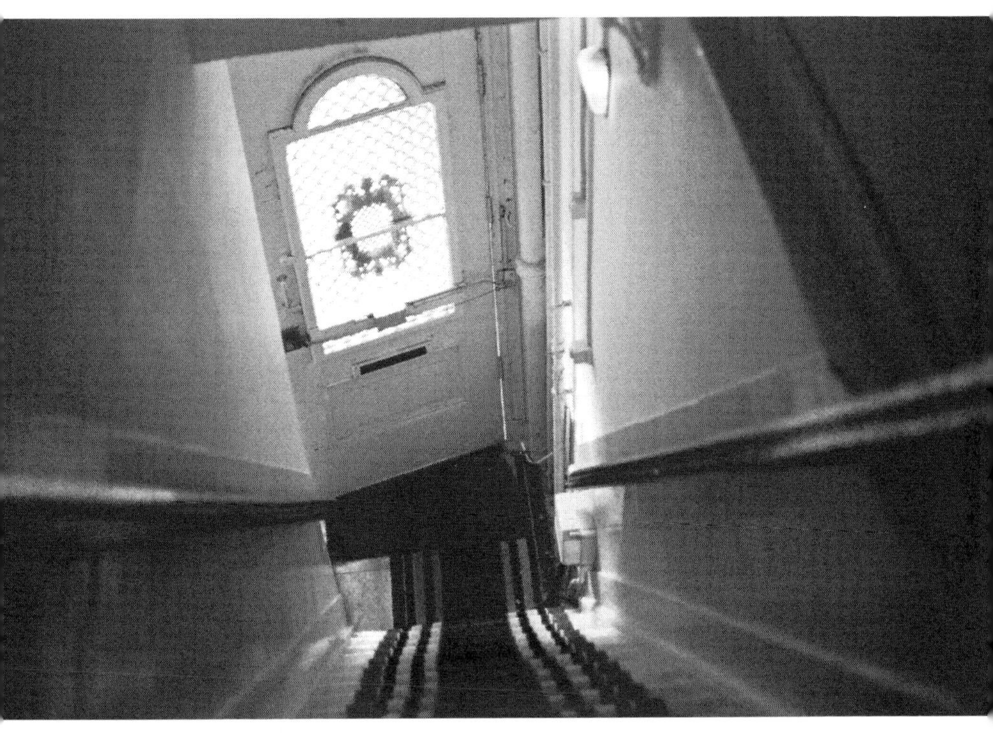

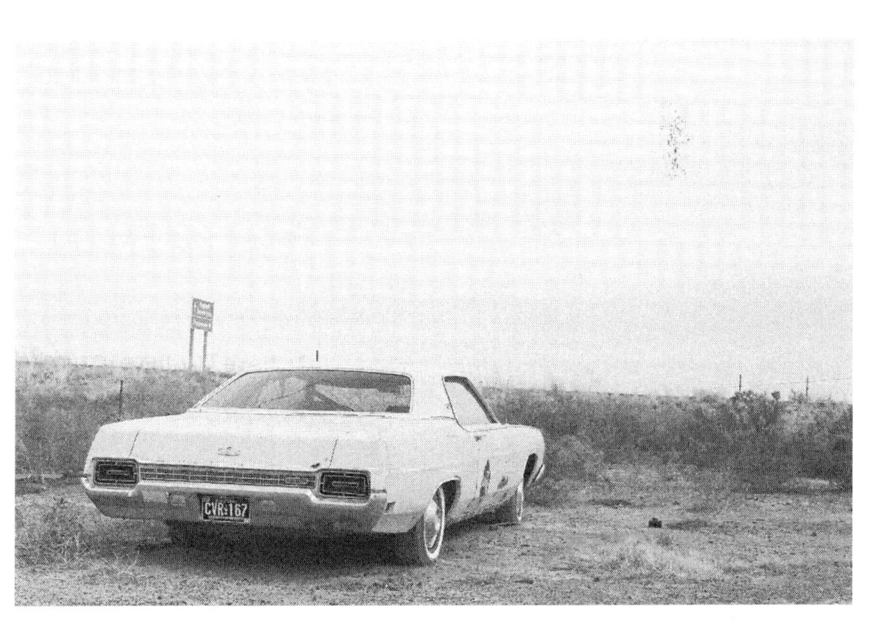

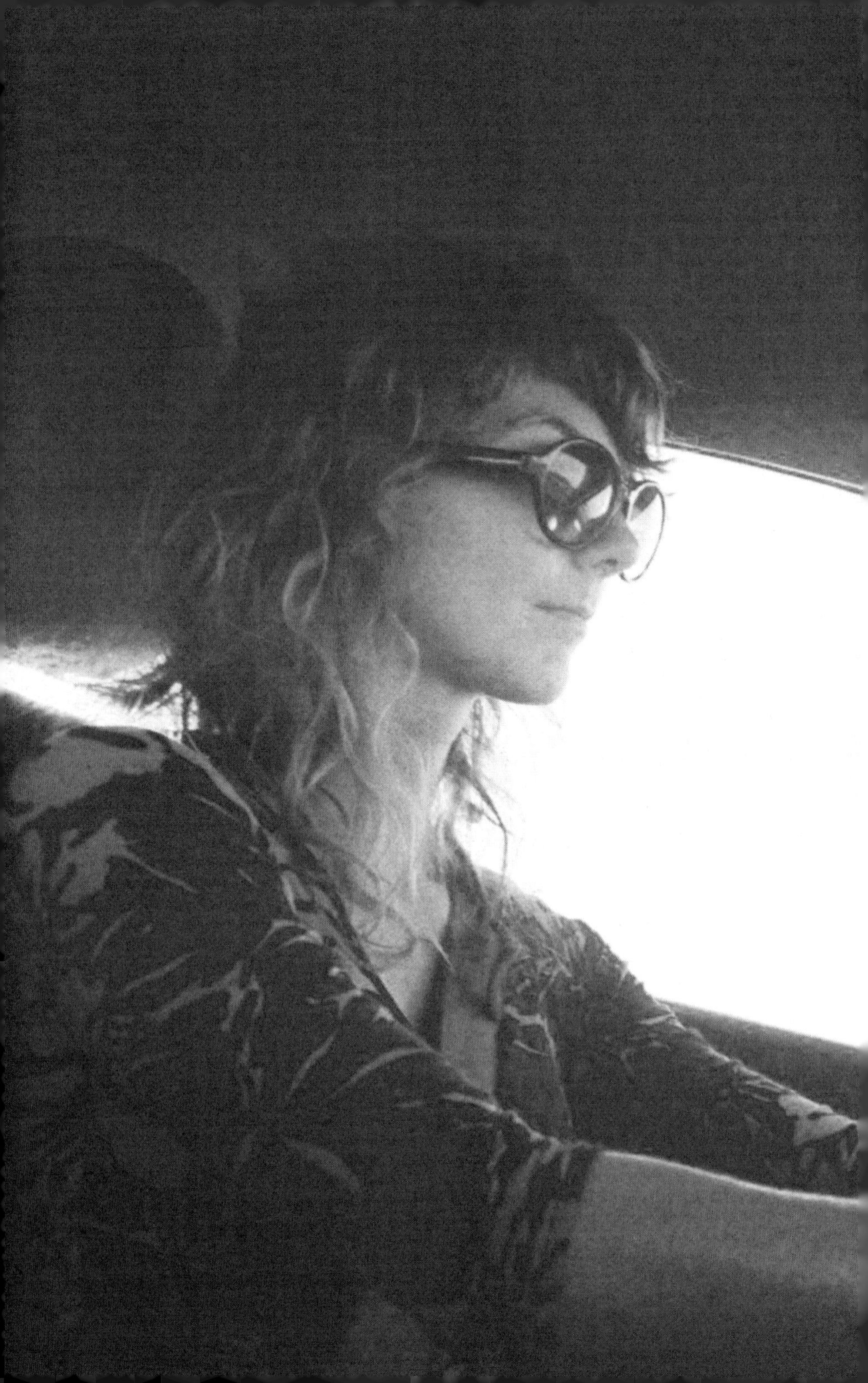

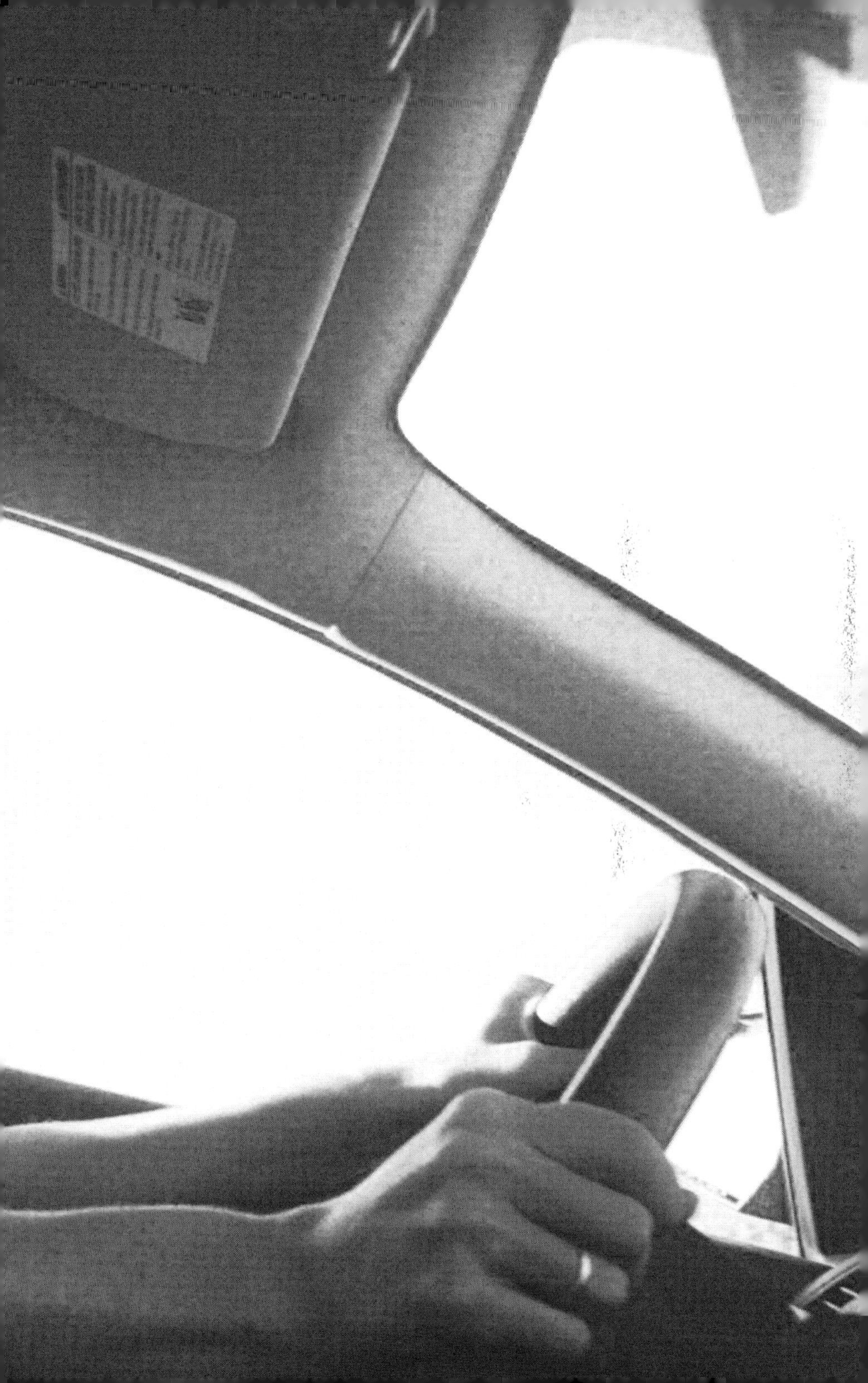

"I hear you're on a road trip," Michael said, pushing the few register buttons necessary to ring up my groceries: some water, some crackers, some cereal and milk.

"Yep," I answered.

"What, did you just read *Eat, Pray, Love* or something?" he asked with a smile.

"Never read it," I said, smiling back. It was clear he was only saying the best thing he knew how, but it still rubbed me the wrong way, revealing something about him that I always hope not to find the first time I meet someone. In his world, an act of independence amounted to drawing within the lines of a box that says "please leave blank." I try to drown the seeds of my contempt with compassion, and half-succeed.

He handed over my change and I asked, "Was it any good?"

"What?"

"*Eat, Pray, Love*. Was it a good book?"

"Dunno," he said. "I didn't read it."

His affable eyes exuded a strong dose of humanity, just benign goodness doused with confusion, and what I think is this: People only rebel in safe spaces.

From a backpack sitting on a shelf behind him, he pulled out a spare key to the apartment upstairs, a place to call home for the next few nights. He shrugged as he handed me the key, explaining that they didn't often lock the door—there was just no need. He led the way to the staircase that ran alongside the building and showed me how to jimmy the gate open in case one of the neighbors did lock it. With a loose wave, a gesture so fluid it could've meant anything from "see you later" to "nothing in this world is worth worrying about," he disappeared back down the stairs to the ground-level convenience store, where he'd be working well into the night.

Michael was a friend of a friend, trusted by word of mouth, though even friends can dismantle and disappoint, so in truth I didn't know what to expect from the apartment. It was a called-in favor. The front door opened into a large living room devoured entirely by couches in various colors and sizes, L-shaped and loveseats packed next to one another, all facing a TV in the corner. The kitchen was large and well-equipped, as so many American kitchens are by default, the counters populated by cereals and health supplements and a smattering of used dishes. Not tidy but clean.

The bedroom that Nora and I would be sharing, offered to us since the guy living there was out of town, had been straightened up, the bed's comforter pulled smoothly to the pillows. Warm sunlight glowed through the vast rear windows, reflecting off floating flickers of dust. It smelled like trees and earth and men.

I landed my suitcase on the floor and crouched to unzip it, but a wayward rolling desk chair pushed my back into genuflect. As I stood up to push the chair under the desk, I saw stacks of papers, bills and notes, pens and staplers, post-its affixed to a computer screen, a small potted cactus, some framed photos of an elderly couple smiling. Evidence of life, of living. A laundry basket, half-filled. A framed poster from a Stevie Nicks concert in 2000. I stepped toward the poster and my foot kicked into something. Startled, I looked down and saw the suitcase. Clothes already spilled over its borders, but still, it was a diminutive thing. The entirety of my portable self, all within the compact frame of a carry-on suitcase.

Nora was sitting on the bed, sorting through her socks, arranging her things into collections of a certain order in little happy stacks. Though I couldn't see her face, the crisp pose of her shoulders was evidence of her smile. The sunlight shone through the stray blonde curls that fell around the back of her neck, the pale skin of her long arms aglow. She looked like a Renaissance painting of a woman symbolizing the comfort and satisfaction of a life well lived at home. Suddenly I could see why the sight of a woman folding laundry was worth portraying, was worth dying for. Wound up in that gentle gesture was the history of civilization, the definition of loving devotion. All the salt of humanity. Maybe my whole life I had been seeking something just so beautiful in its simplicity. She looked over her shoulder, and as our eyes met I realized I'd been staring, though she didn't seem to notice. She said, "Do you want to go into the city to find some Mexican food before going to the museum?" and the moment was lost, if it ever existed.

"Sounds good," I said, turning back to the desk.

In my apartment, a stapler was the foreign object, but here... It wasn't the stapler that was out of place.

The abyss came rushing toward me, that vertiginous darkness that pulls me down, down... I kicked my suitcase closed, shoving it a little under the bed with my foot and said, "You ready?"

Nora wrapped her small bag over her shoulder and gave a pert nod of enthusiasm: She, too, was ready to go.

Twelve years I'd been gone. How much more time needed to pass before I stopped thinking of it as being "gone" from somewhere and started counting something else instead? Seven years in Amsterdam. Thirty-four years alive. One day in San Francisco. Three weeks till I go back. One second for one breath. Another.   Another.   Faster. I try to hold my breath in, but it won't stop. Time escapes through my lips.

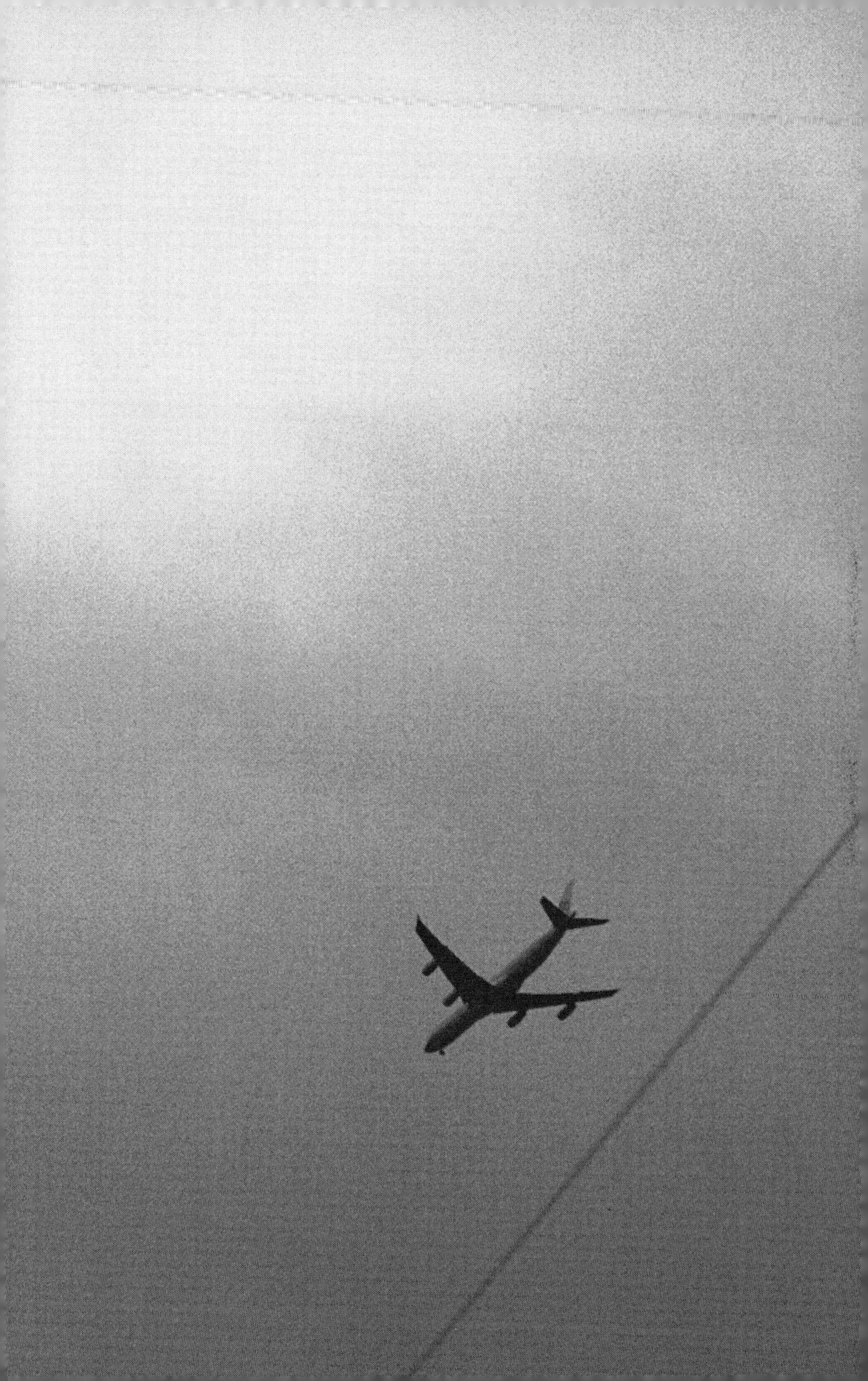

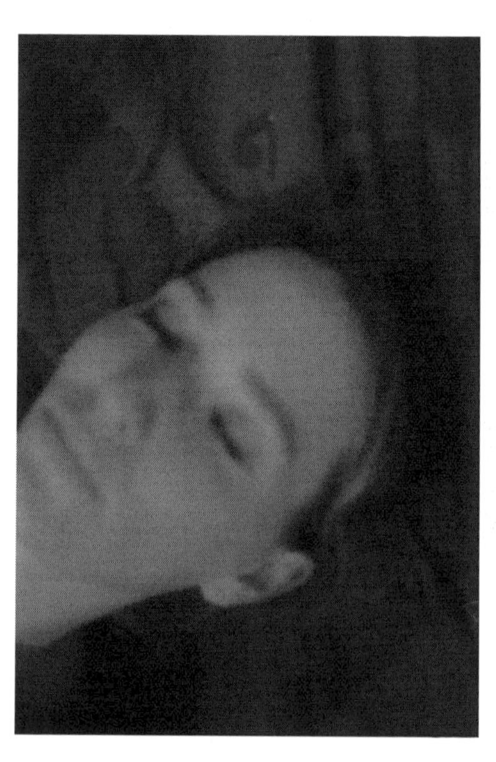

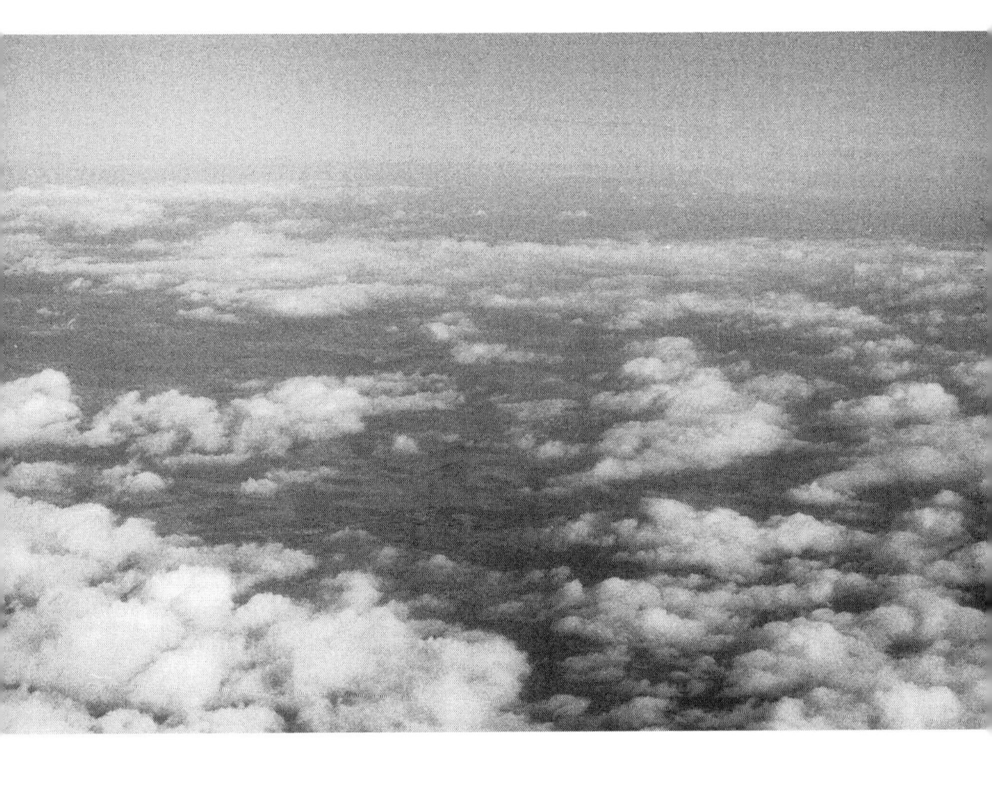

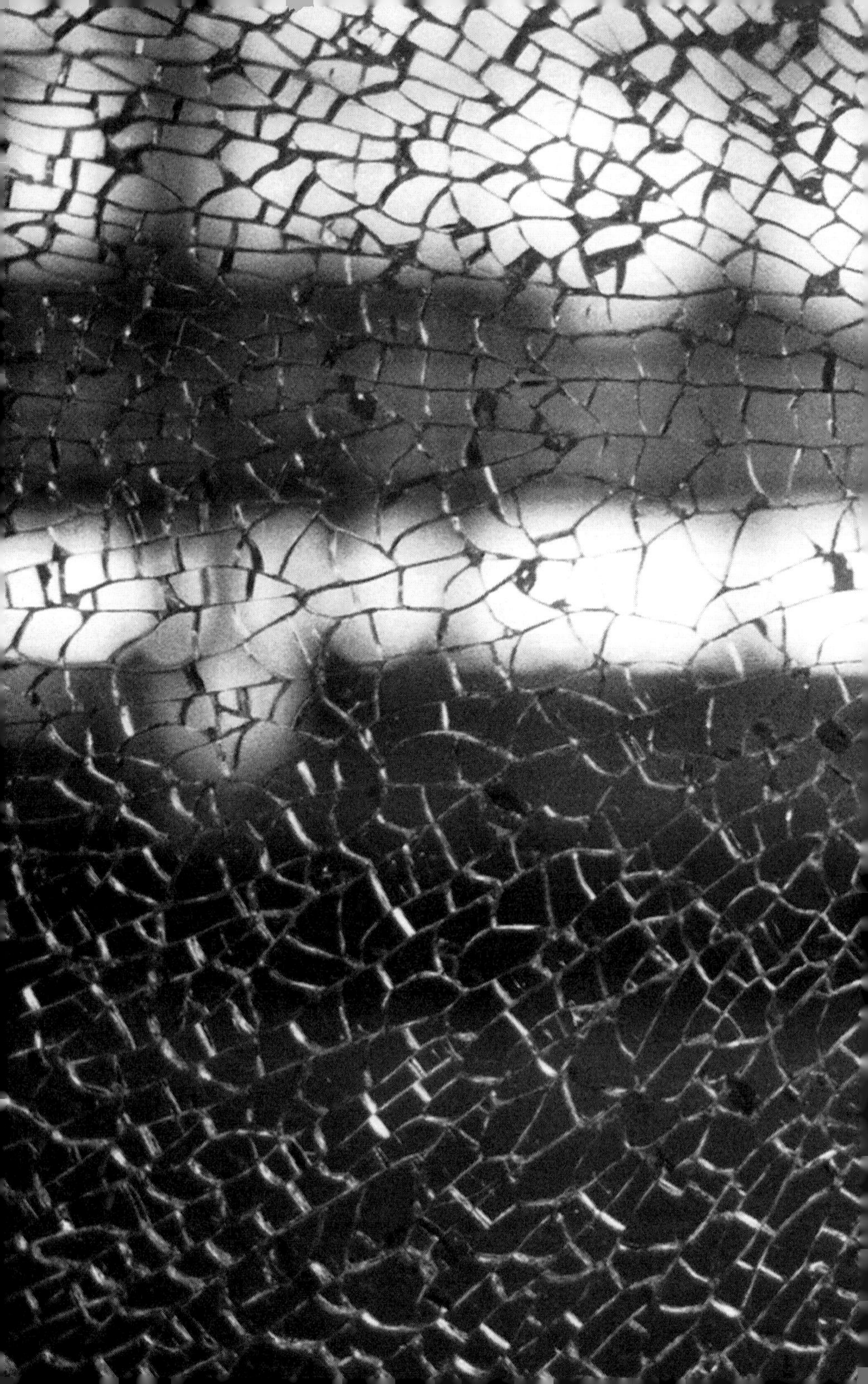

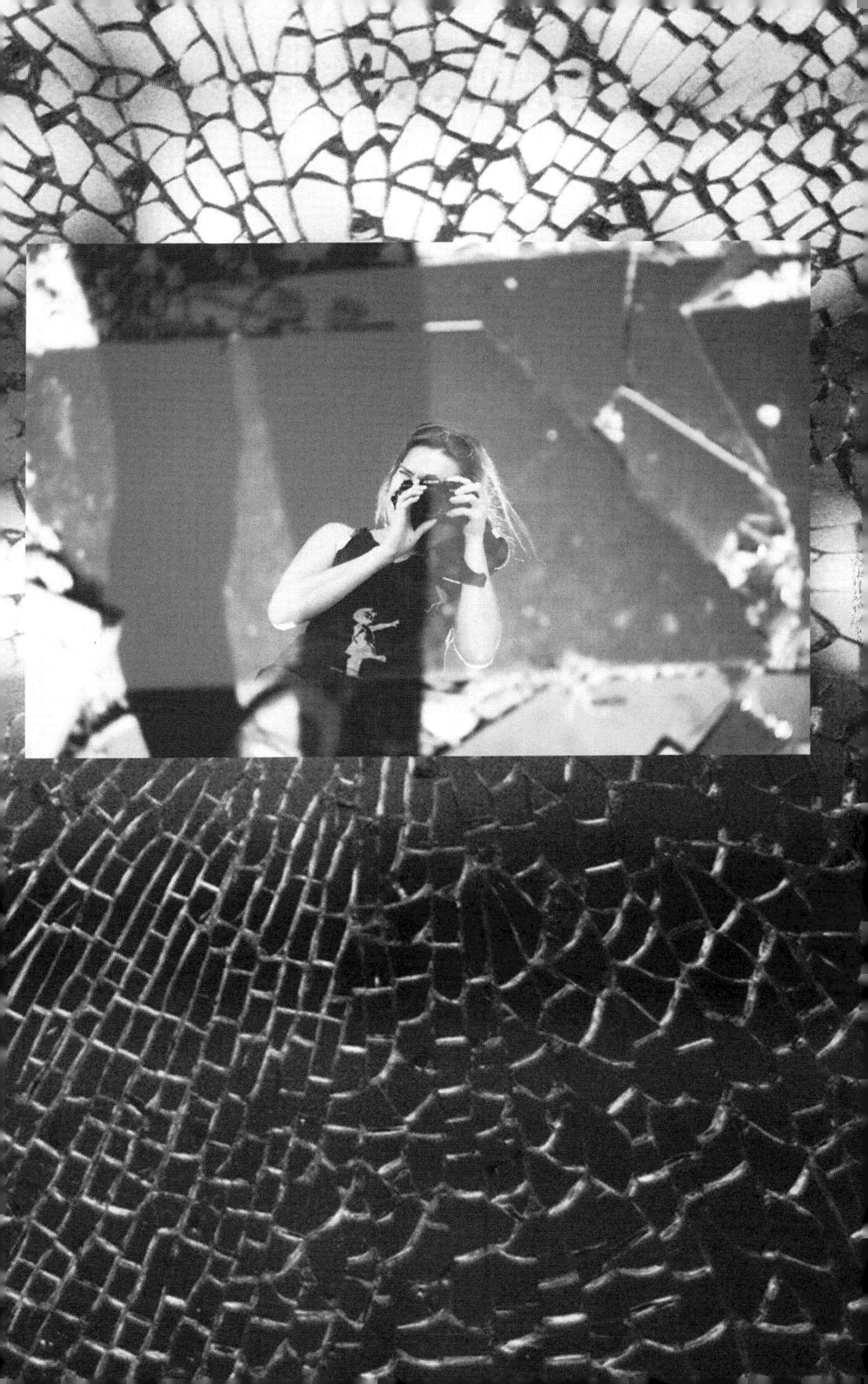

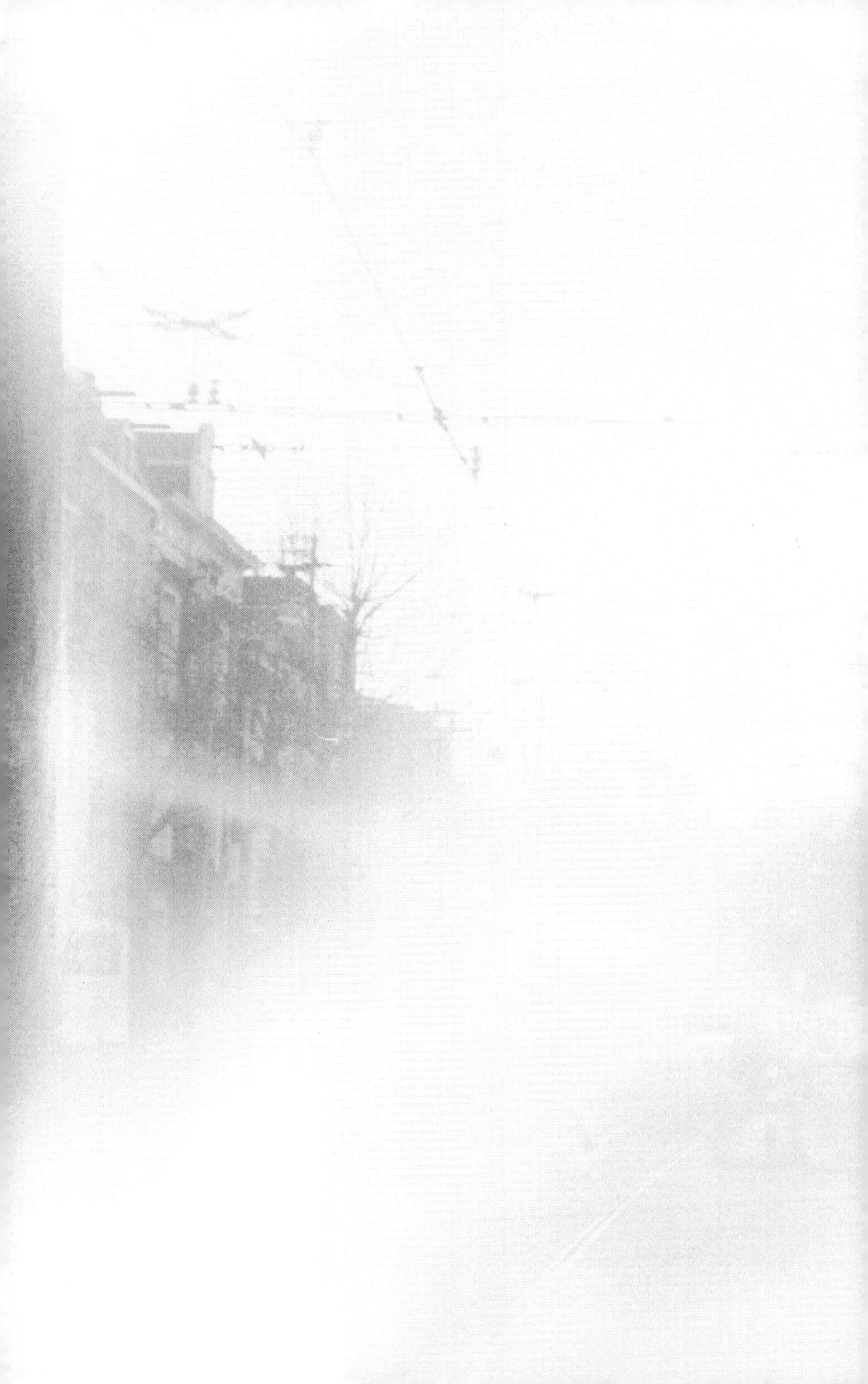

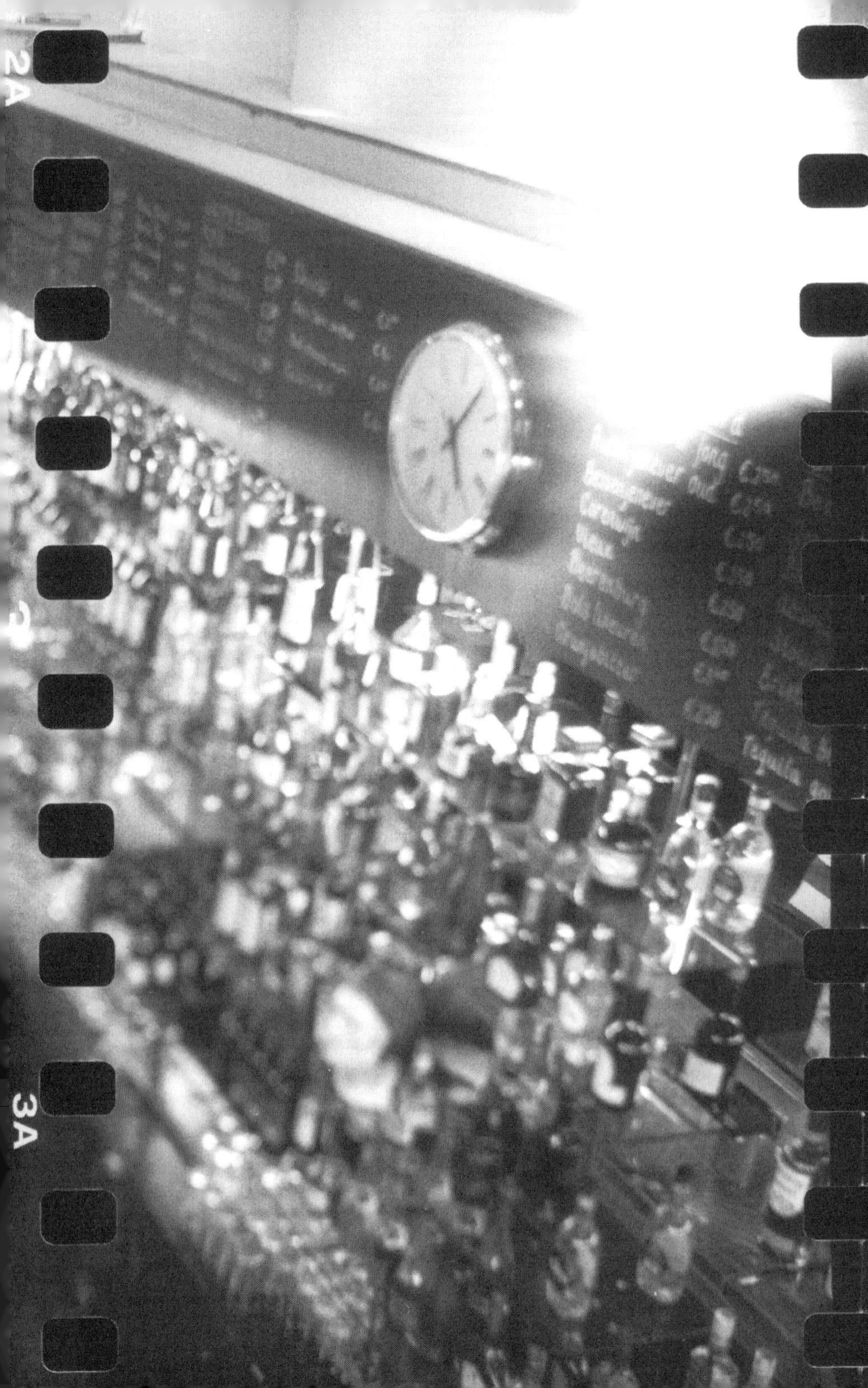

"When I went to Bangalore the first time," Mark continued, picking his beer up, swilling the final third of it and then setting the glass down again, "it was for a business trip, so I didn't have much time to explore. I really only got to see the parts of the city between the hotel and the office."

"That's a shame," I said, wondering how many trips to Bangalore I'd need to hear about. "Do you know—"

"—But the next time I went, that was all for me. And what a phenomenal experience! When I came back to Amsterdam and walked around the city again, I thought, my god, we're so privileged here."

I nodded, hoping it wasn't the first time that he'd realized he was privileged. "It sounds amazing," I said, already picturing the comfort of my bed as I curled up under the covers and listened to the rain drumming on the roof, unstoppable. I tapped the lacquered bar a couple of times, and even though I couldn't hear anything over the vocal roar in the background, I felt it in my fingertips. "And anyway, it's great that your work paid for the trip. You probably racked up a ton of air miles."

"Oh absolutely," he said, obscured by the shadows of the dimly lit bar. He leaned forward, his head crested by the overhead lamp. "And this was still during the boom period, so I flew in business class. Give me a Bloody Mary on an early morning flight and I have no complaints at all!"

I thought if he meant it, that he really had no complaints, then his privilege extended into depths of self that I would never be able to fully grasp. "I think it's time for me to go home," I said, trying the words out, seeing how they'd sound out loud.

"One more before you go?" he asked, and I said okay because the thought of "no, I've already had too much" got slurred in my head and turned into "why not?"

He asked for another round of beers from the bartender, who I casually observed was more attractive than Mark, and I realized the only point of any of this — the drinks, the conversation, the man — was to avoid going home.

"*Proost*," we said and clinked glasses. I took a sip and tasted nothing but cold. I mentally made a list of every place I'd rather be than here, reminded myself of the heat of Valencia, the buzz of New York, the flirting of Palermo.

Mark continued the story of his visit to India, which he thought made him special and I nodded and pretended that it did, even though there are hundreds of flights a day. "It's really quite remarkable there," he said with the characteristic Dutch version of English, a crisp punctuation of distinct words, the emphasis sometimes falling strangely on the wrong syllable. "I would love to go back and spend a few months there. The people are so amazing, if you consider that they've really got nothing at all, but they're so resilient, so smiling."

I took another sip of beer and tried to feel something like alive.

Everything went blurry and I excused myself. I worked my way through men and women much taller than me who all seemed to be wearing the same thing even though they weren't and pushed open the bathroom door. I slapped cold water on my face and looked in the mirror for some kind of consolation, but the answer came back: *Sorry, I've got my own problems.*

I blinked, and the water droplets that had collected on my eyelashes descended my cheek. I turned away.

The overpowering brightness of the room brought with it an unwelcome visceral clarity, but I didn't blame the light. It only fulfilled the function required of it. Light tells you where you are. I thought of the timeless tension between literal and metaphorical light and dark. Plato's man in the cave allegory. If man were born in a cave of obstructions, where all he ever knew of other men was their shadows, but then one day got to see another man in light, to see the "truth," could he ever go back into the cave and see only shadows?

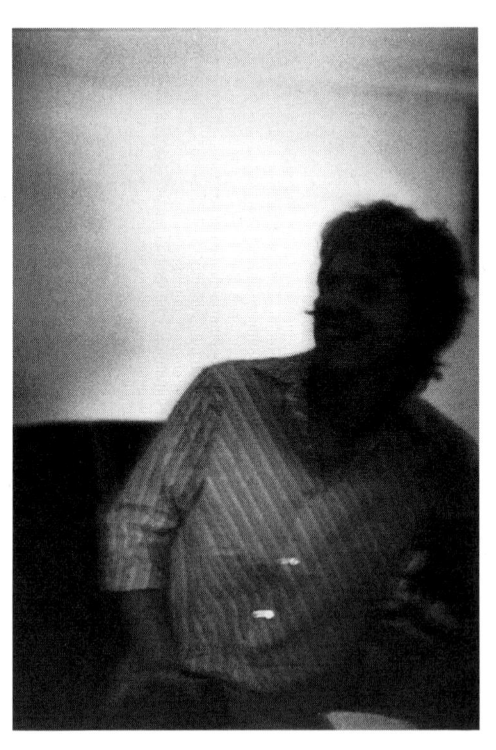

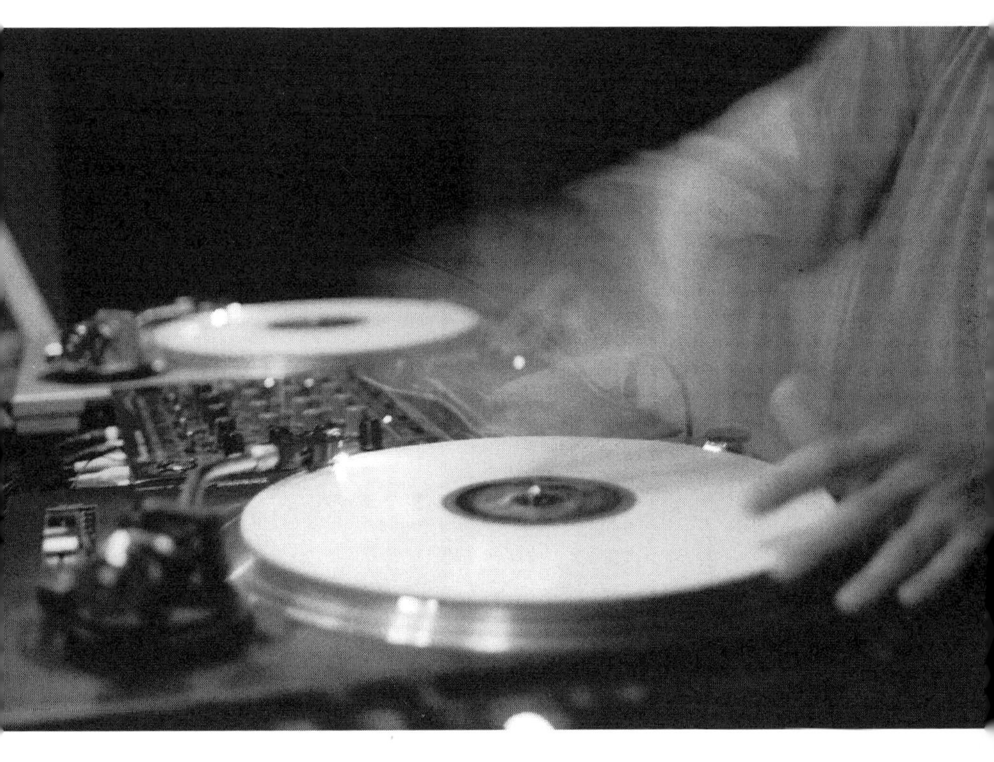

The shadow of a man is the tabula rasa of our imagination. I'd known so many shadows that were greater than the man who formed them.

The sharp lighting of the bathroom told me I should be able to see things accurately. The dimly lit bar told me to fill in the blind spots with whatever I wanted. Complete dark could be danger or safety, just depending.

I opened the door back into the buzzing madness of a Friday night, voices echoing around the room, ever increasing in volume, individuals indistinguishable. Making my way back to the barstool, I passed groups of men who in any other country might have looked at me, might have spoken, but here in Holland had co-selected their role as the pretty birds, the lure.

Mark had taken out his phone to click out some correspondence or otherwise escape himself. I sat down and he finished a couple more taps before putting it back in his pocket.

I don't mean to say that Mark wasn't an interesting guy, but this might be a good time to mention that his name wasn't actually Mark. I can't remember his name, so let's call him Mark because it's friendly and generic, a good name for a prototype of a person you meet once. He was interesting enough to have a conversation with over a couple of beers, it's just that, so is almost everybody in the world. On any given night in any given city, I could start talking to anybody and have an okay time. Some people like to take that personally. Maybe I do, too. We were both insufferable, suffering each other together.

"Okay!" I said, holding my hands up in the air. "Lightning round. Favorite bar in the world. Go."

"Okay, ahhh..." he said, his eyes lit up as he searched the ceiling of the bar for the right memory. "Sky bar. London. The bartenders there are fantastic for cocktails."

"I do love a good cocktail," I said. "But I'm going to have to go with view over taste. Berlin TV tower. 207 meters off the ground."

"What was the view like?" he asked.

"Fuck if I can remember. Okay, bad answer—No wait! I know. The bar at the top of the Park Hyatt in Tokyo. The one from *Lost in Translation*. Really weird cocktails, great view."

"Did you go before or after the movie?"

"After. It's kind of ridiculous to go to some expensive bar just because it was in a movie, but it was just so iconic. They made it seem so cool and boring."

"A bar for rich cynics!" he roared with laughter. "Sounds perfect for me!"

"I kind of wished I was staying at that hotel but, hey, I wasn't traveling for business," I paused to take a sip of cold nothing. "I might like to live at that hotel for a while. It would be awesome to live in a hotel, like a John Irving novel."

"Who?" he asked.

"American writer," I said. "Doesn't matter."

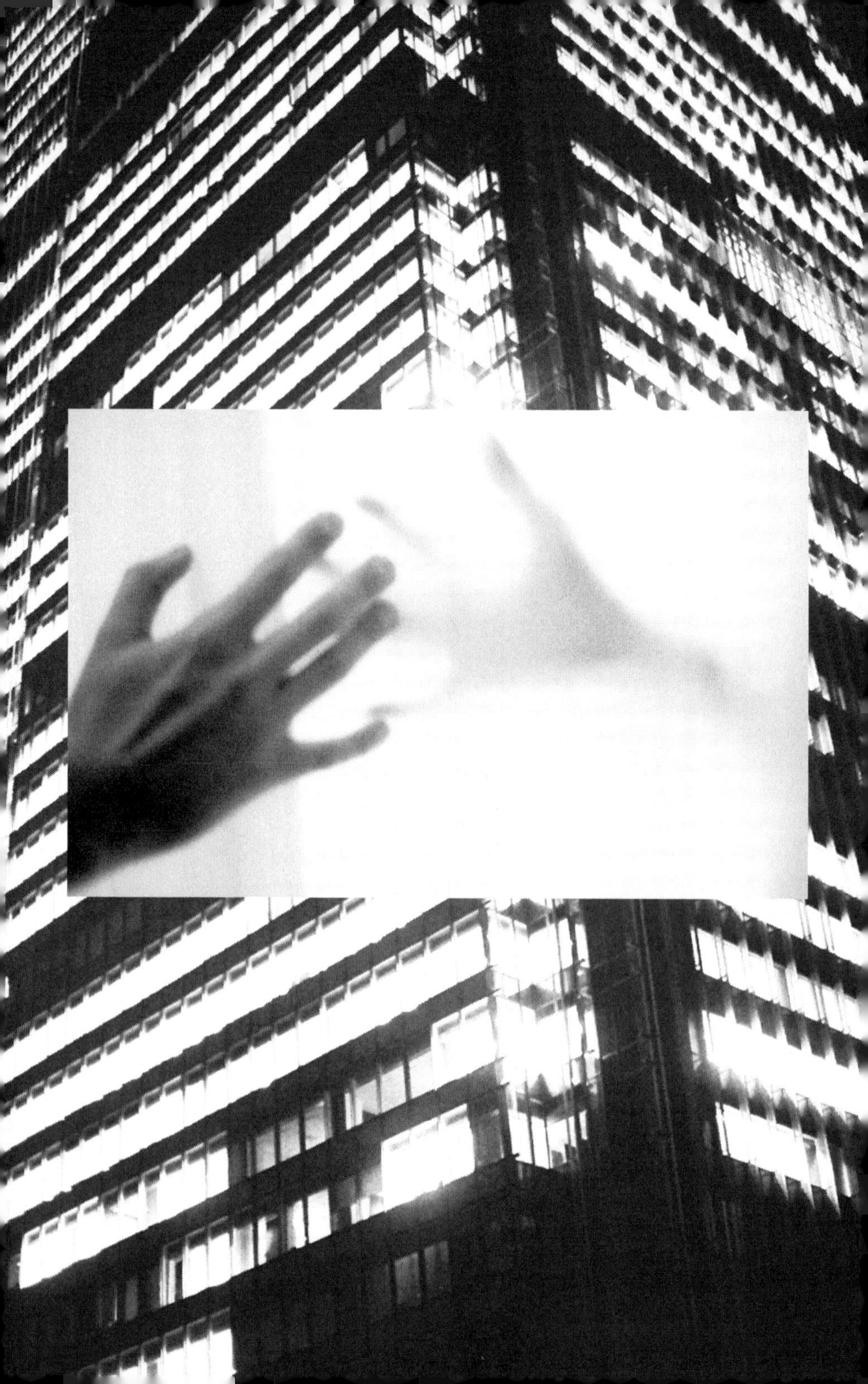

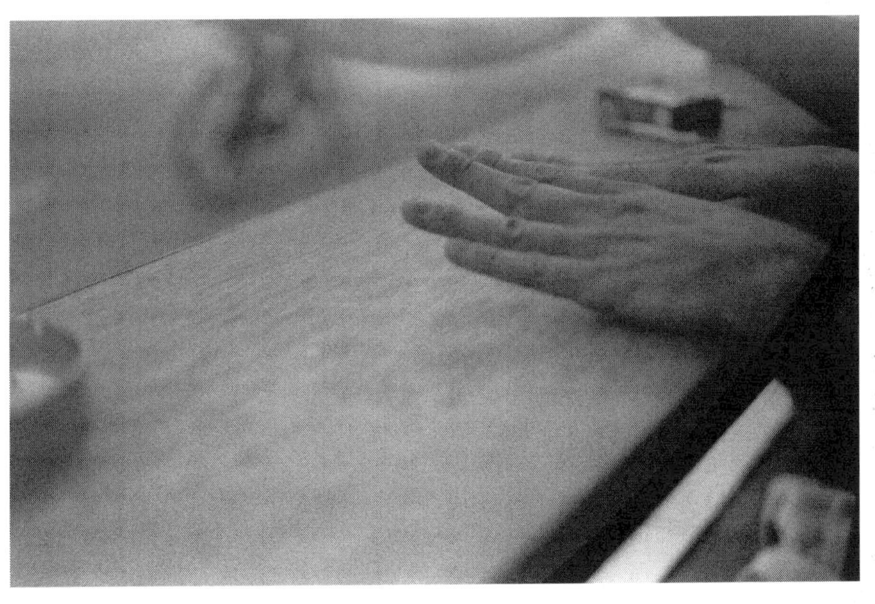

Mark told me a story about staying at a hotel in Barcelona where he caught a maid rifling through his things, who then denied everything so convincingly that he ended up apologizing to her. He only realized his passport was missing when he got to the airport. His face fell into and out of shadows as he spoke. Occasionally his head would tilt back just so, and the small lamps above the bar would light up his eyes like periwinkle watercolor on a black and white photo print. Just for a second. Then it would shift again and his whole face would be drenched in the red indirect light of a dark wood bar. His hands would be hidden by shadows and then visible as he took a sip, light then dark, light then dark. Blanks that I could fill.

"I wouldn't want to live in a hotel," he said. "They're so impersonal, the towels are kind of like sandpaper. I don't like hotels at all, actually."

"Me either."

"But you'd want to live in one?"

"Yeah," I said.

"That doesn't make sense," he said.

"Best beach. Go!"

"Oof," Mark squinted. "I'm not one for beaches, but the diving in Egypt is fantastic."

"Sounds like a lot of work," I said. "I'll wait for you on the black sand beaches of Tenerife."

"Highest point on the earth?" he asked.

"Same place actually! Tenerife. I went to the top of El Teide."

"For me, it was the Himalayas. You should really go to India," he said, steering the conversation back to his own area of expertise. He gave my shoulder a bit of a punch, then grabbed it firmly, shaking me back and forth for emphasis, the kind of clumsy gesture of casual violence I'd come to understand as the Dutch version of flirting.

His sweater was nice. It didn't have any beading or loose threads. Just a nice dark color with a collared shirt underneath. He carried a bit of extra weight in his face and chest, the pro forma figure for an office man, but that was ok. It bothered me more than anything that he looked like a cardboard cut-out of a "Dutch man": his golden hair, slightly long and curvy, brushed back with more gel than really necessary, paired with jeans and pointy brown shoes. I watched his lips move as he talked about trekking mountains with some vague notion that he was probably fuckable.

I thought again of the warmth of my bed and waffled between the urge to stay and the urge to go.

The problem wasn't with the place—my apartment in Amsterdam or anywhere. It was something else, elemental in my making. I don't know how we all agreed on the idea of Friday, for example. Going out on a Friday. There's more to it than a long history of labor laws establishing the standard of a weekend, or even back beyond to the biblical notion of God's day of rest after working.

There must be tied up inside us, along with an instinct to breathe and eat, something that informed the idea of work and reward. And even deeper than that are the parts we can't quite understand because we never see the whole, the patterns of behavior that together form a hive of humanity, complementary and reactive. A vibration that causes some to obey, some to rebel. Some to create, others to destroy. Some to seek company, some to seek solitude. Always just enough of everything, balancing. Somehow, we perceive all these things and adjust ourselves, all the while defending our choices as something that we *want*.

I found myself swaying, like there was a wind I wanted to listen to, and I remembered Alan Watts describing that we do not come into the world but out of it, like leaves on a tree. Where was the tree that none of us could see?

Some unseen force called upon me to pursue a course called "an individual" while the nature of such a thing, laughably, depended on others to define itself. My refusal to belong anywhere, to have a home, depended on all those places I didn't stay. It was a choice I made again and again even while knowing it was not my own. I listened to the universe that resided inside me. I obeyed my branches and roots.

Mark's face fell once more into darkness. What vibrations of human instructions was he receiving?

"... And that's the problem with outsourcing," he said, finishing some thought that I hadn't heard. It was all so banal until all of a sudden it wasn't: "It's good that people are so different from each other, but it takes time to understand."

I flinched at his words, the way he completed a sentence I wasn't saying. Were my thoughts even mine, or were thoughts just signals in the ether, out there for anyone to pick up and interpret through their meat-bound biology?

My balance slipped, making it clear that continuing to sit upright on a stool would be a challenge. The last beer had finished me. I stood up and said, "I'm going to go. It's late."

He stood up with me and said, "Yes, good idea. I play squash in the morning." He put on his jacket while I put on my raincoat, and we stepped outside into the constant winter drizzle.

"My bike's over there," I waved my hand in the direction across the street.

"Mine's just here," he said.

"It was nice to meet you," I said, leaning in for a generic Dutch goodbye, a quick succession of three alternating cheek kisses.

Instead, he took me brusquely by the shoulders and kissed me firmly on the cheek, just once, then held onto me, asking questions with his eyes.

"Why would you want to kiss sadness?" I asked, pulling myself away and stumbling toward my bicycle.

"Good night," he called out, unflappable or oblivious.

I rode home in the midnight air and black night, with bicycles pedaling in formation along the arteries of the city. My fingers were already frozen against the handlebars as I reached the bridge that would take me across the Amstel into the eastern part of the city. I pedaled hard up the angle of the bridge, hit the center as the street lights flickered reflections across the water, and then let gravity pull me down the long, fast slope, the wind and water rushing cold across my cheeks and running their chilly fingers through my hair. I stopped at the light at Wibautstraat and waited, drops of water beading across my knuckles, the rain saturating my jacket. I heard the empty streets echo with a distant bike bell or shouts of laughter, and though the city made sounds around me there was finally the beautiful silence of being alone. There were no one's expectations bearing down on me to be a certain way and no obligations to keep up my end of the conversation. All the voices in my head even, that clamorous pack of flamingos, had been sedated for a spell.

I never met anybody who wasn't tormented in some way by the voices in their head, demanding or diminishing, and I was no different. Most of the time, those voices were a lot louder than anything else going on. But then there were times exactly like this, exactly now: living and so alive. Not trying to be but being. Feeling the pulse of life beating through me, not as my own heartbeat but as something bigger than myself, that told me it was all okay. Rain knew how to fall without me telling it to. Birds knew how to fly, spiders knew how to shape their thread into webs, trees knew how to grow, planets circled the sun. And me, too—I'd know what to do without needing to figure it out. I sat apart from all the things I'd done, all the things I'd make, all the things I needed to become—I was just living and living and living.

And then, just as quickly as the feeling arrived, it fell away and I was back in my head on the wet winter streets of Holland, pedaling in the dark toward home.

Home was a comfortable thing. But in comfort nothing rattled. And all the interesting parts of life, all the growth of character and moments of sublime insight and bloodlettings of intense joy, they all took place outside of that comfort, someplace in proximity to the rattling. That's the trouble with comfort: It gets you wishing that the whole world would stop moving, that all the people and birds and stars would stay just where they are, for you. It's something a little bit like death.

It was the pursuit of all golden things that filled one's eyes with light. Things that, once possessed, lost their luster.

I climbed the four flights of stairs to my apartment, unlocked the door, and two round, blinking eyes reflected the hallway light that poured in behind me.

"Did I wake you?" I asked and was met with a meow that turned midway into a long, reaching yawn. I shut the door and stood in the dark. I heard some furry rustling and felt a soft body curl its way around my leg. I knew that I could find my way without counting or feeling, without fear, just moving through the space that was mine. It was a warm and comfortable death.

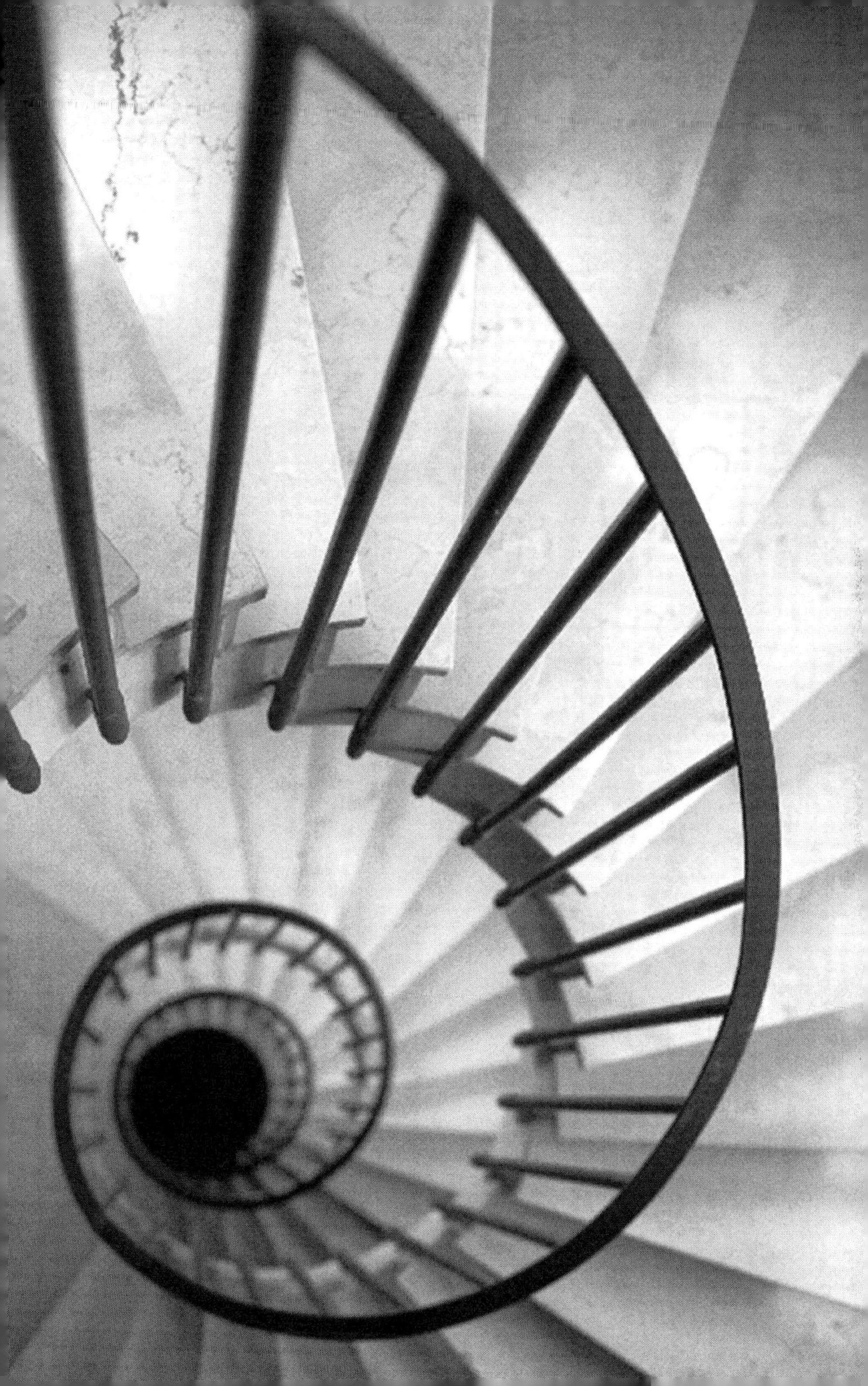

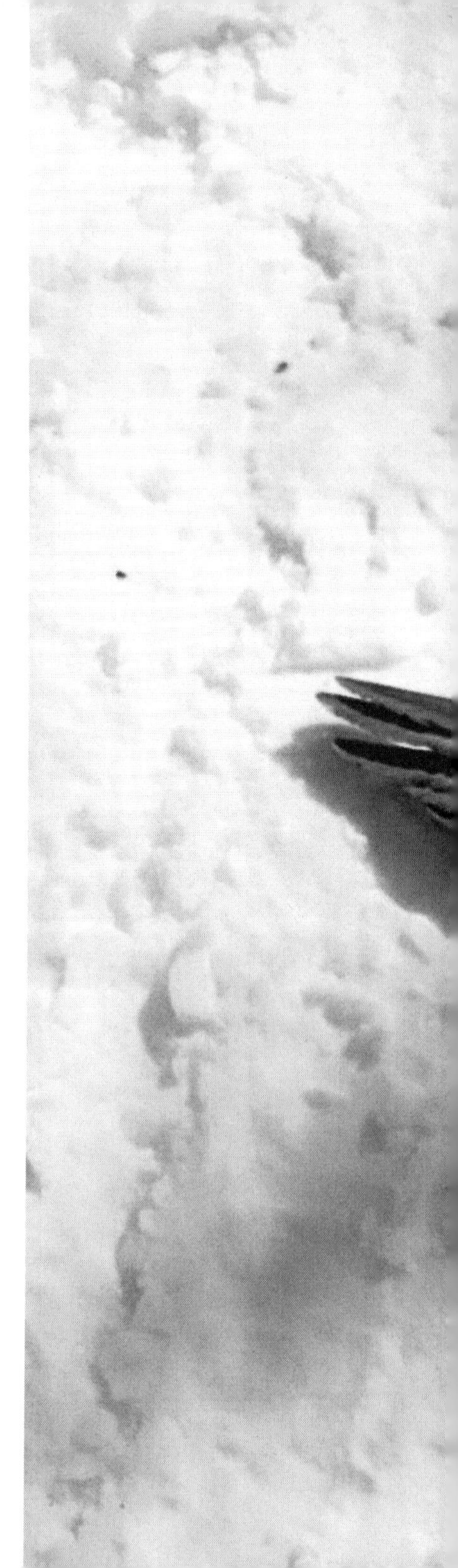

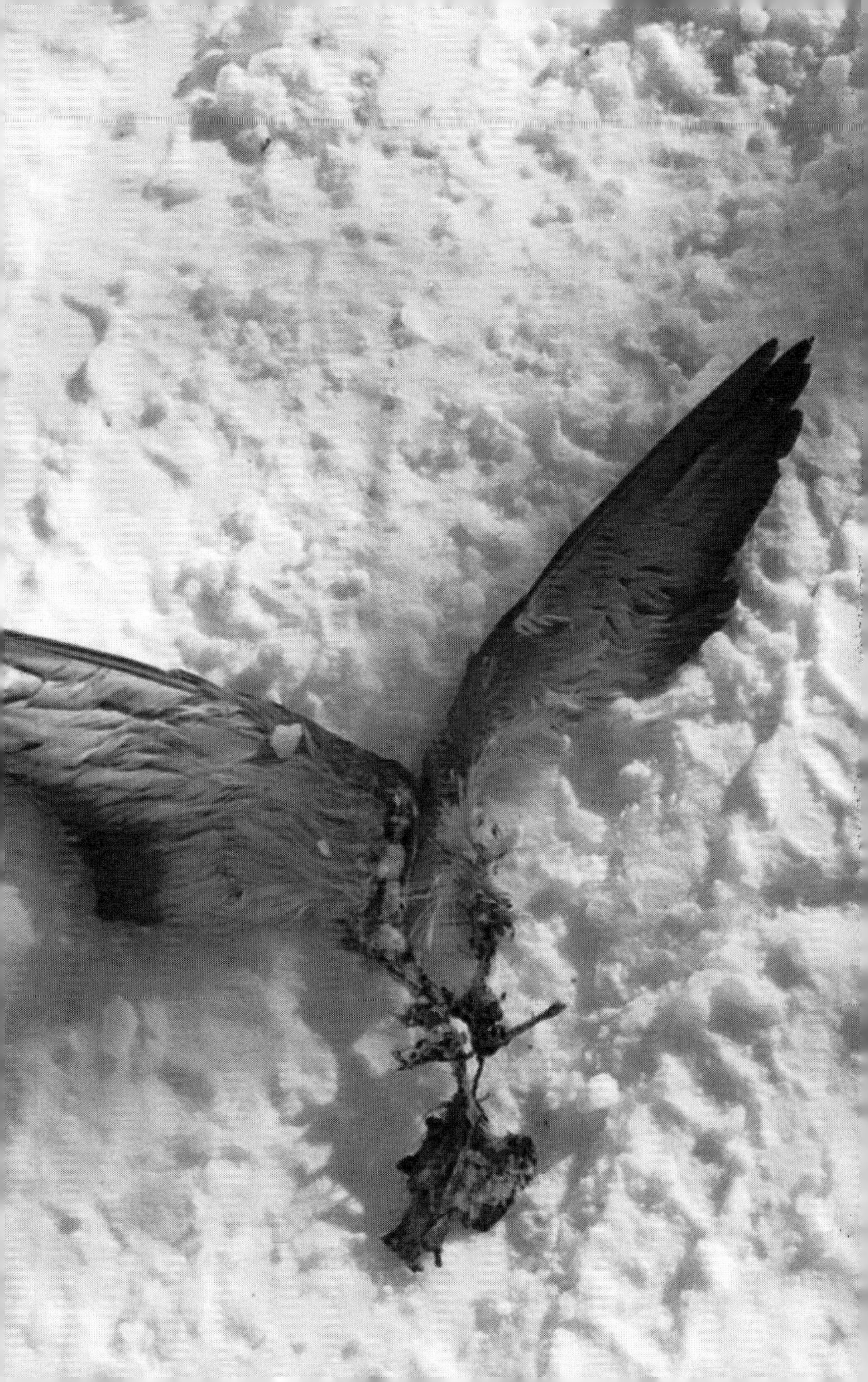

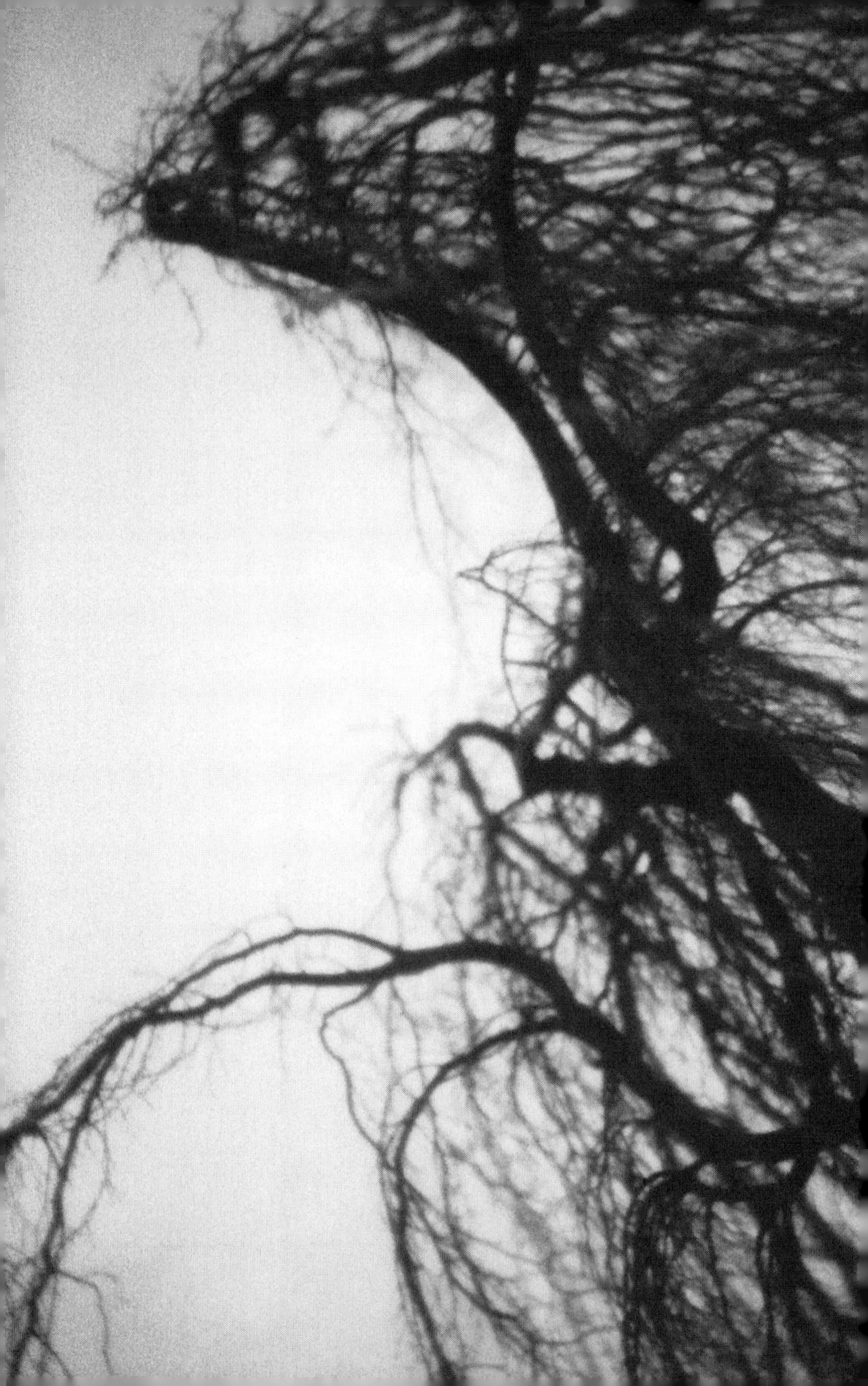

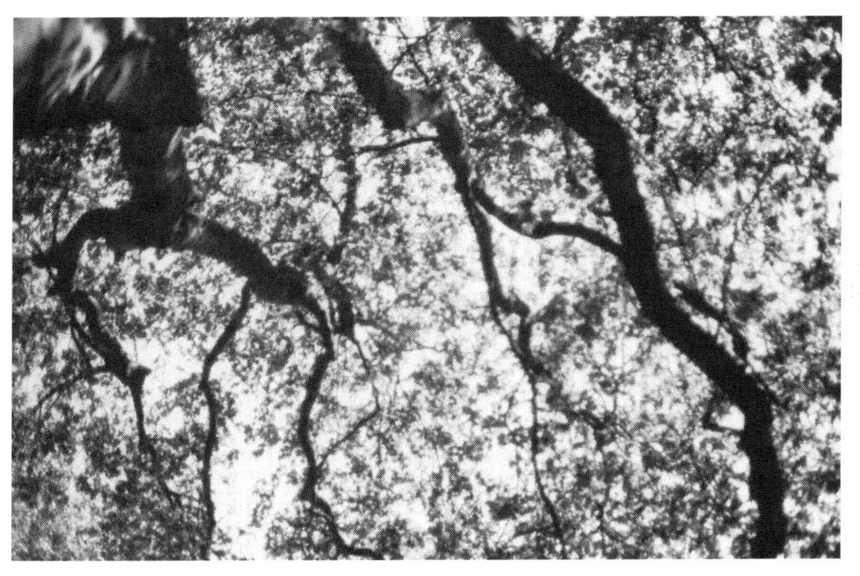

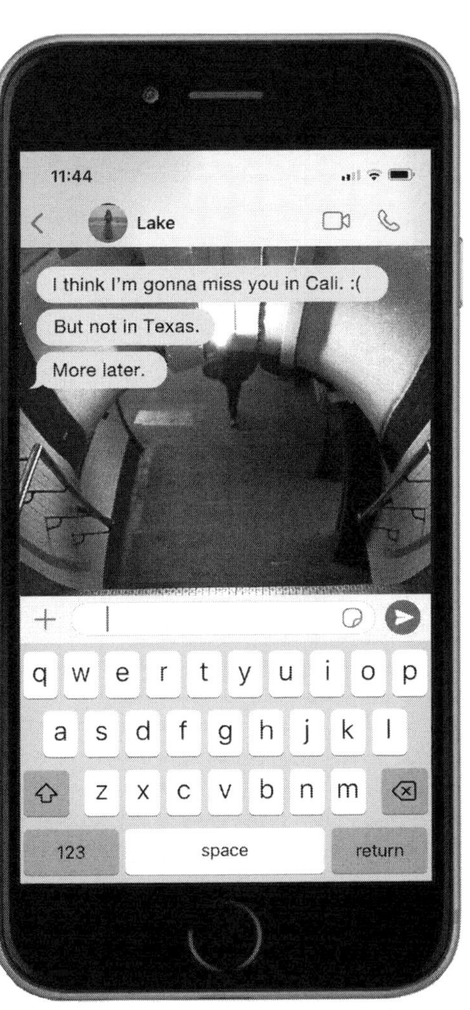

11:44
Lake
I think I'm gonna miss you in Cali. :(
But not in Texas.
More later.
q w e r t y u i o p
a s d f g h j k l
z x c v b n m
123
space
return

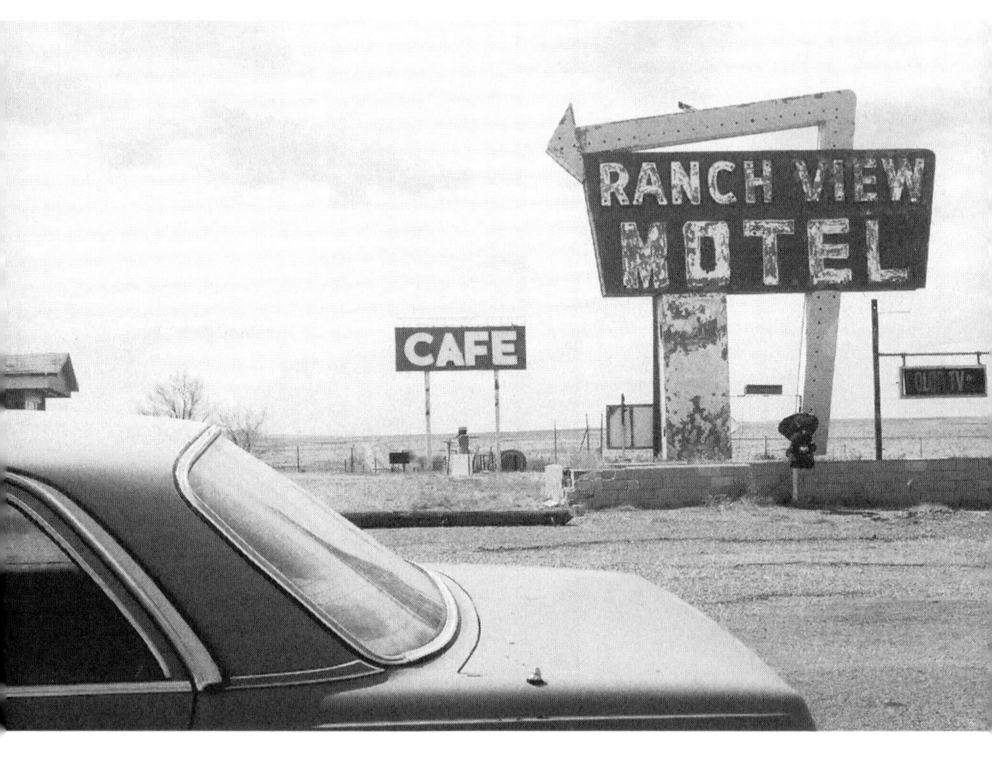

RANCH VIEW
MOTEL
CAFE

We've been chasing Lake since San Francisco, which only sort of makes sense considering she's trailing us by around three days. Supposedly, she's the one trying to catch up to me and Nora, but the thing is, I know when she's left to her own devices she'll forget about time. It was one of the pleasures of her company, to be sure, a slowness of calm that made you feel in the wrong for rushing.

When I picture Lake, I see her singing on a small stage in the bar of a modern hotel. Out of place but making it hers. She had a summer gig, and was wearing a flowing white dress, tapping a soulful rhythm with her bare feet against the unfinished wooden boards. Her muscular arms, long and dark, held a guitar with an easy insouciance. Her singing poured out slow and rich like chocolate, something to be savored. So even though she's behind us, it's still us following her, ahead of time, round the southern curve down to Texas.

Sitting in the backseat with us is the sorrow that comes from chasing someone who's already behind. I keep thinking it shouldn't be this way, a refrain that grows into an irksome ticking in my ear like cozying up to a wristwatch. There was only a half a day's difference between us when we left LA, which felt so close we might've touched, but once we hit desert, it was straight through without slack. Lake wouldn't be doing the same.

We get to the hotel in Williams and Nora takes a picture of me while I brush my teeth, saying: "This is what you look like when you brush your teeth in a hotel in Williams!" I check the screen of her camera and admit to her it's more interesting than I thought it would be. Something about the moonlight coming in through the lace curtains. Maybe something about the confident curve of my back as I stand in the second-floor window, overlooking the drag like I own it.

When we wake up in the morning, the desert sun is already shining through the window frills, and in the sobriety of daytime our room resembles a grandmother's boudoir, with ancient, frosted-glass light fixtures and porcelain decorations. I'm struck down by the morning melancholy of being on the road, that awful feeling of having been still for long enough to realize that the thing you thought would make you happy won't, that happiness is a horizon destination, something to be chased in futility like a setting sun between mountains on a curved road. I feel the intense urge to sleep again rather than confront my thoughts on the matter. Brains should come with an emergency shut-down button or a steam valve, but they don't, so we have alcoholics and psychotics.

I take a shower and avoid eye contact with the

needy depressive in the mirror. I refuse to be an alcoholic, which means my only option is psychosis. My grandmother was a schizophrenic, so I've always watched my thoughts suspiciously, picking each one up aggressively by the scruff and interrogating: Are you the son of a bitch that finally proves I've gone and lost it?

Watching people from the outside, most of them look so normal. I mean, if they manage to dress themselves and buy groceries and can carry on a five-minute conversation without shouting something obscene, that pretty much takes care of most worldly interactions. Maybe if people were more willing to talk about their workaday demons, it wouldn't fill us with so much anxiety of being exposed.

"I feel like my face is drowning," I say to Nora from the bathroom. She's perched herself at the desk and is typing on her laptop.

She smiles and says, "Just your face?"

"Yes, just my face. I can breathe everywhere except my face."

"That's okay then," she says. "You can't judge people by their faces."

I nod, affirmed, and return to the bathroom to put some makeup on the face that can't be judged and, because it can't be judged, feels less like drowning. I mess up my eyeliner, and I'm glad I've been granted immunity from judging. Nora, like everyone, looks normal but isn't.

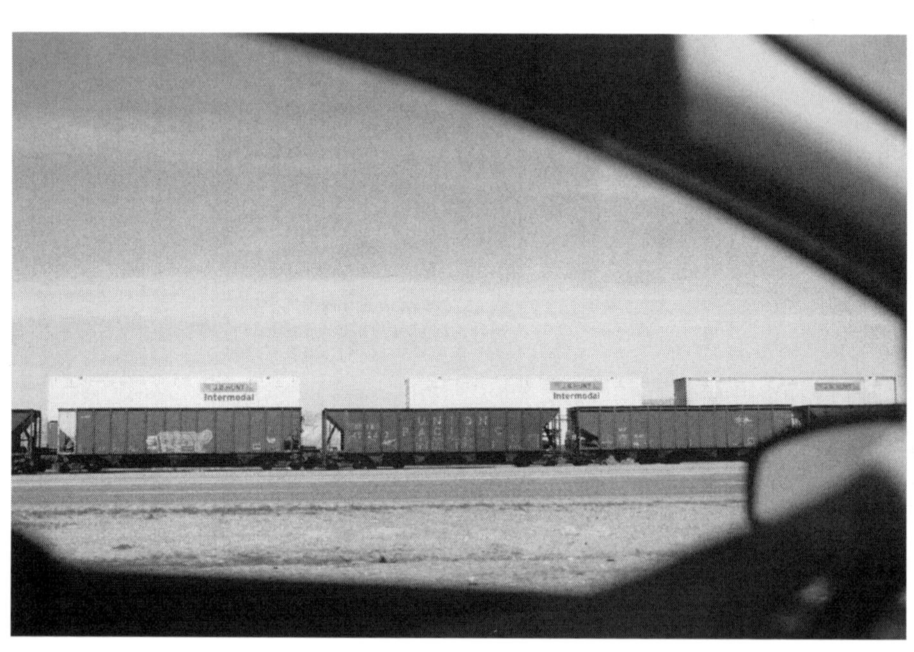
Intermodal
Intermodal

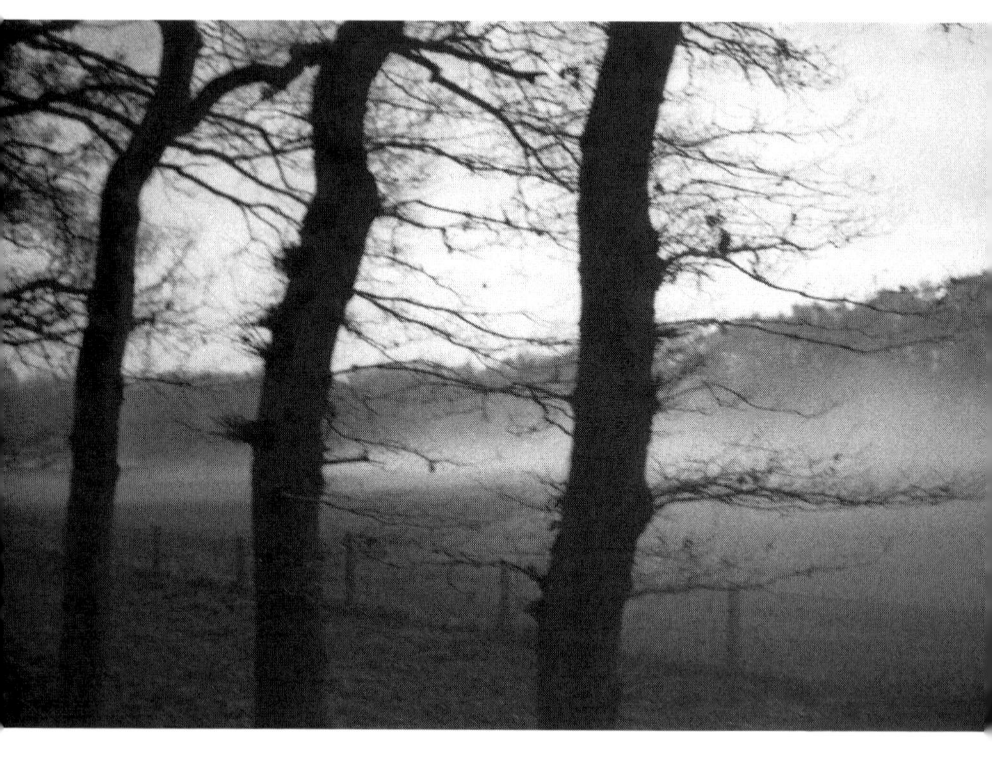

I think of
an artist
like a
CAGED
TIGER,

pacing back and forth across the country of her enclosure, roaring her discontent.

And how she must love the walls of that enclosure.

We're driving east along the old Route 66, which isn't anything special now, just one more nightmarish highway of many in a connected country, but one thing is forever the same: When you are urged from within to keep moving, there is no such thing as arrival. One road just introduces you to the next.

This particular road trip leads to Houston, where I'll take a plane back to Amsterdam. A series of roads leading to an airport feels like an ending, or maybe a beginning, while in fact it's neither. Everything carries on, in every direction, all the time. Freedom isn't choosing between a couple of alternatives, it's authoring order from maelstrom.

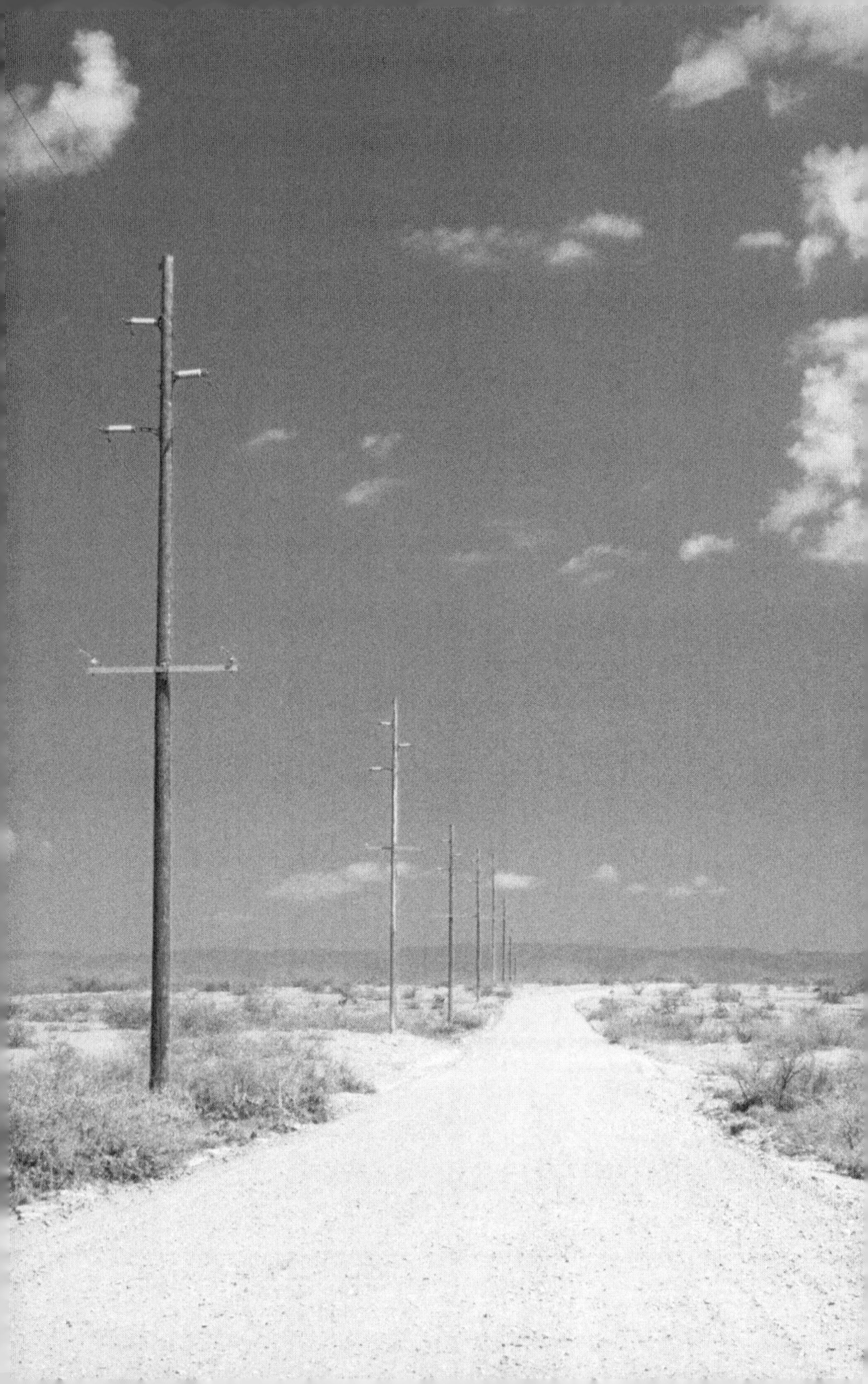

It's a lot easier to react to order that already exists, and that's what I mean about the walls. There is no zookeeper; the tiger constructs her own constraints. I never saw it, never felt it, until the moment I had finally cleared from view any worn paths, creating a life that was mine truly, and realized in a panic that I was not yet done roaring.

Into the infinite, I roared. The empty echo had nowhere to go but deep inside, exposing a loneliness of such despair I can't bring myself to describe it. A roar turned inward finds all weaknesses, all fears. But should that tiger find a way to put some walls up... my god, there are so many things to roar about. What sweet release.

I can't deny I love the dusty roads of nowhere, the abandoned buildings that have moldered away like dreams upon awakening. Emptied gas stations with signs announcing prices from long ago, their histories as readable as lines in rocks or trees. As I drive along the highway, hour after hour, I leave thoughts behind, gratefully.

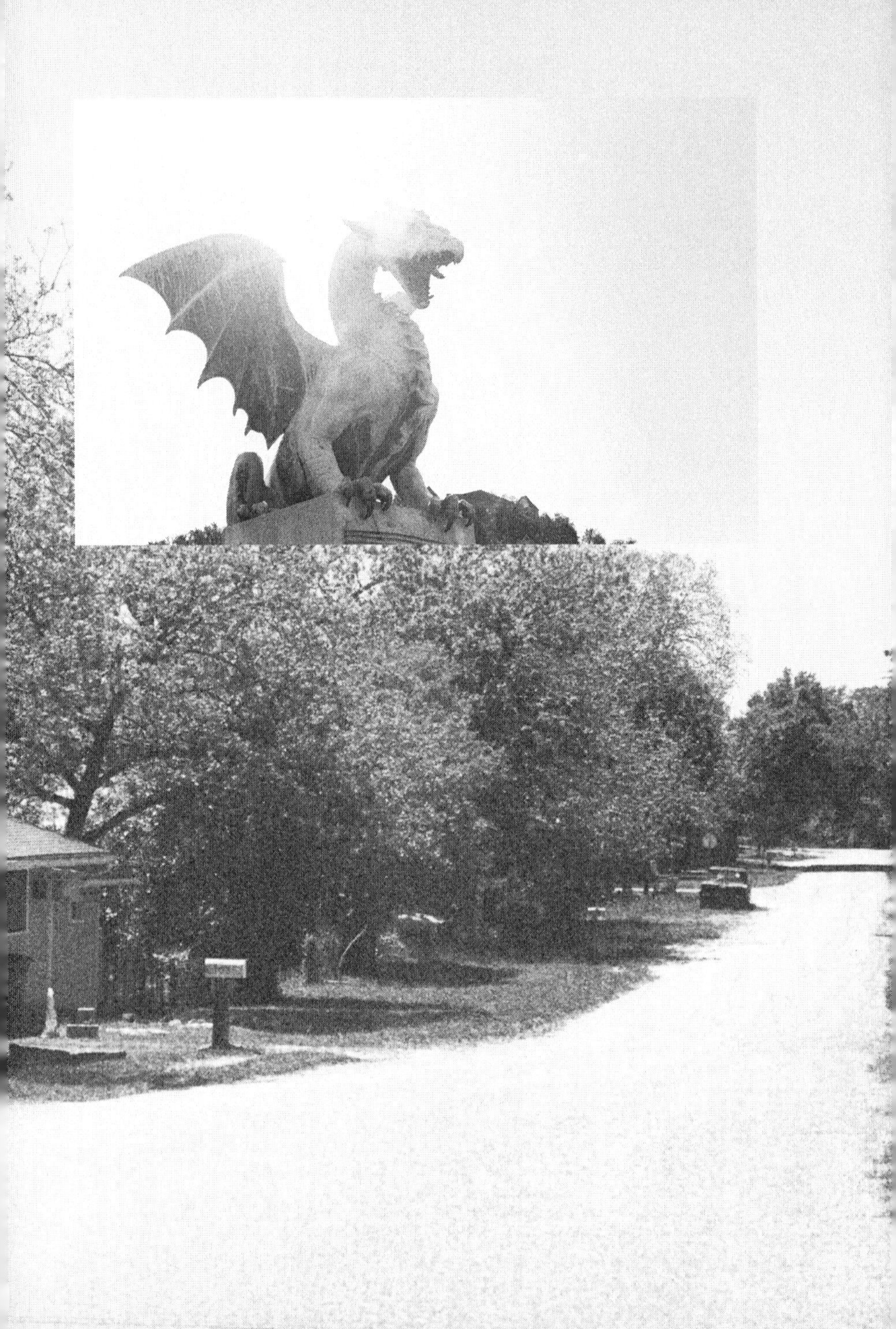

Though these never-ending paths can so easily feel like exploration, their very existence is evidence of civilization developed far beyond wayfinding. I can feel their well-worn grooves draw me in with man-made gravity. Roads court direction, pulling this way more than that. They beckon with their explicit limitation, reassuring. The 66 was built on the myth of American freedom by car, as though adventure ever came with a gift shop.

I pull off to refuel, and have my choice between two gas stations, one on each corner.

Cars pass by, going to countless destinations all in the same direction, and I lean against the trunk as the pump clicks into action. Listening with my eyes closed, the smell of gas oppressive.

Still as I am, my mind starts calculating a list of things needing my attention back in Amsterdam. When I read Kerouac describing the periods in between trips, they're abbreviated and take on a tone like he knows they're dead weight, the boring parts of life that we all know happen but nobody has any interest in reading. But is domesticity really where interest goes to die? It's where so much of life happens, in that time between home and gone again. I go to work, I see friends. I write. I sleep and go to the movies and sit on the couch petting my cats. All that shit readers don't want to read about but that happens, too. There's more of it, even.

But the movement is what captivates. The act of building a cage and roaring in it.

Meanwhile, true to zoo form, others spectate. The artist enacts her dance of furious liberty, fur wild and heart open, and records it so that others can read it and through her pages receive vicarious assurance that they, too, are capable of great adventure, of untamed autonomy, of a heart

beating
bloody.

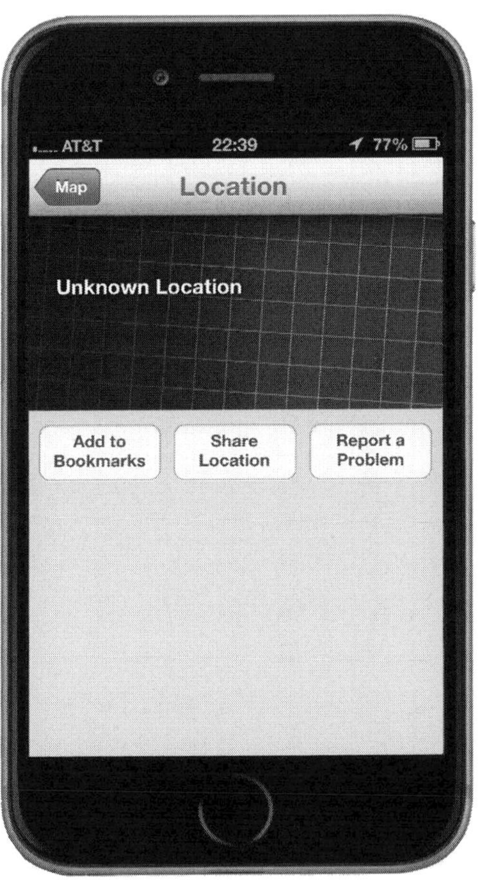

We've been cruising for a couple of HOURS

through the long-winded yawn of West Texas, and hard in the throes of highway hypnosis I'm brooding about betrayal. With dust in all directions and oil jacks pumping like clockwork, I can't wait to get gone, but the numbness of my ass tells me it's time to stop. I muse aloud into the silence, "I might stop the car soon."

Nora nods.

Miles and miles of nothing. It might give the impression that there is in fact nothing, but that's not exactly true. A dirt drive will turn off unannounced into an area enclosed by a barbed-wire fence and it's apparent that even though it seems the same as all the other nothing, someone regards it protectively. There's no explaining love.

We come to a handful of buildings that might've been put there by accident.

In the middle of this abbreviated town, we find a Mexican restaurant cuddled on one side by a shuttered former shop and on the other by a strip

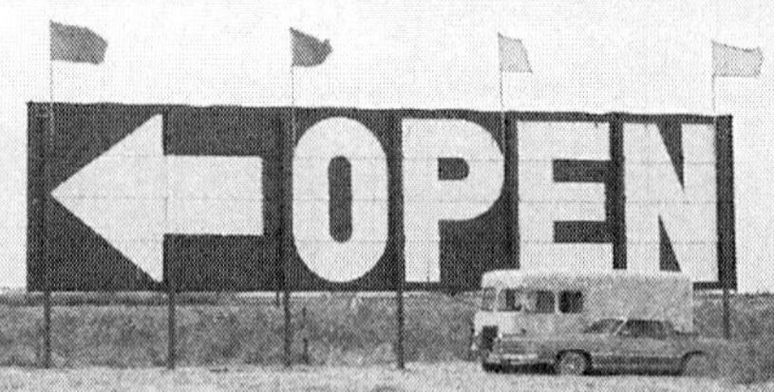
OPEN

club named Candy's. The windows are darkened by what could be called limousine tint. It's bubbled, cracked, and peeling, but the effect is intact: You can't see inside.

I squint sidelong at Nora because I'm having second thoughts, but I don't think we'll reach any kind of clarity for another couple hundred miles.

We shrug our way inside.

The place is lit, barely, by the bit of daylight diffusing through the windowed wall, like the glow of a TV from a neighboring room. Track lighting offers inadequate support from above, and wood veneer ceiling fans circulate air and dust with an arrhythmic bump-bumpity-bump, bumpity-bump. Two old men, each sitting alone, glance up briefly to gauge us then turn back to their own tables.

Nora and I take a seat in a booth, and a defeated woman limps over to us with a pad of paper in her hand. We both order a coffee and I ask for the menu, which seems to surprise her.

The silence of the place is unnerving. I look up from the laminated menu and realize one of the diners has left. He didn't make a sound; he was just gone. Maybe he'd never been there.

The waitress returns with the coffees and two oversized tumblers of water with straws. The end of each straw is covered by the torn-off tip of its paper casing, the simulacrum of sterility that fools no one. She places a basket of tortilla chips between us, along with a little bowl of salsa.

The coffee is both bitter and watery, and this is what finally breaks me. I keep trying to drown the coffee with creamer to make it drinkable but just end up in a loop: Futile effort and fail, repeat.

I mumble, "I work too much."

Nora brushes the tips of her fingers along her lips. "So, why do you work too much?"

I hesitate. Some answers take a lot of unfolding. "Lake told me once: A lover is a bucket with a hole in it."

"Are you saying that work is like a lover?" Nora asks.

"No, I'm saying you've got to have something else to fill up the bucket."

The waitress arrives to deliver the chiles rellenos we'd ordered and I eat one aiming for comfort, only to be reunited with failure. The cheese is chalky, the spice has been fried to oblivion, and the oily batter falls to pieces in my hands.

I eat another one out of defiance and continue: "I'm saying it's not just that the bucket has a hole in it, the bucket is thirsty. I put the fucking bucket down, but it's following me around, sucking me dry. And I keep fighting, I keep working, just to get some energy back, but the bucket sucks it out of me. It's not just a hole, it's a black hole. This bucket has gravity. I'm totally empty. And maybe the scariest thing of all is that I can still walk and talk like a living person. I still do laundry."

"You seem all right to me," Nora says.

"What do you think a person who's falling apart looks like, Nora?" I ask, the disorder coming to life like a suitcase thrown onto a dusty wooden table. I cough up some unspoken disaster of a decision, swallow it hard with a sip of ice water. "Skin hides a lot," I say, "it holds things together. Like, this man I told you I was in love with. The married man. It wasn't just that my entire moral system was turned inside out. I mean, it's a real headfuck to live out a complete discrepancy between your beliefs and your actions, but it's more than that. The things he told me... the romantic shit he filled my head with. That's a poison that you have to bleed out."

She nods and tilts her head, the corners of her mouth curving up in consolation. She starts to reach for another fried pepper but then her hand diverts to pick up her coffee instead.

"They're usually better," I say pointlessly. "The rellenos."

"I'm not that hungry anyway," she says.

Who was the owner of the betrayal? I wonder. Who betrayed who? How many guilty parties were there, and what does guilt mean, anyway? It's not like I slept with the guy, it was just mutually assured destruction by immaculate wanting.

No, let's not be so naive as to throw the word "love" around like it's the summer breeze.

It comes with a cost when we say to someone, "I love you," but we may not find out its true cost until later, much later.

I didn't feel like a fool for the things that happened, because we agreed to take that leap together. Again and again, he made it seem like the weight of his fall might be more than I could handle, far greater than my own, and he kept asking me for my readiness. He didn't just ask me to love a married man, he asked me to be okay with the consequences of breaking up a marriage. He didn't just ask me to love children, he asked me to be willing to swallow the loathing of step-children. He asked me to be okay with being the bad guy. Again and again, he asked: Will you love me enough to do these things? He asked that of me. He asked.

And, betting the whole of my heart on black, I agreed. I jumped. I fell.

I choke down a regret of coffee before continuing: "I poured everything I had through the hole in that goddamned bucket."

Once someone has asked so much of you, once you've asked so much of yourself, more than you knew you even have, how do you pick yourself back up? How?

"But you can't really be empty, you know," Nora says.

"I can't be empty?"

"You haven't lost anything because you're still

here. See, you're here in front of me. I'm looking at you now!" she says, radiating.

I nudge the salsa with my forefinger. "So, what if I'm not *empty*, what if I'm just salsa with too many tomatoes? Basically... I'm tomato sauce. Even though I still know that I'm supposed to be salsa."

"Maybe the world needs more tomato sauce." Nora furrows her brow and sets her cup of coffee down with finality, saying, "This coffee is really not good."

"Agreed," I say, putting on my sunglasses. "Let's get out of here."

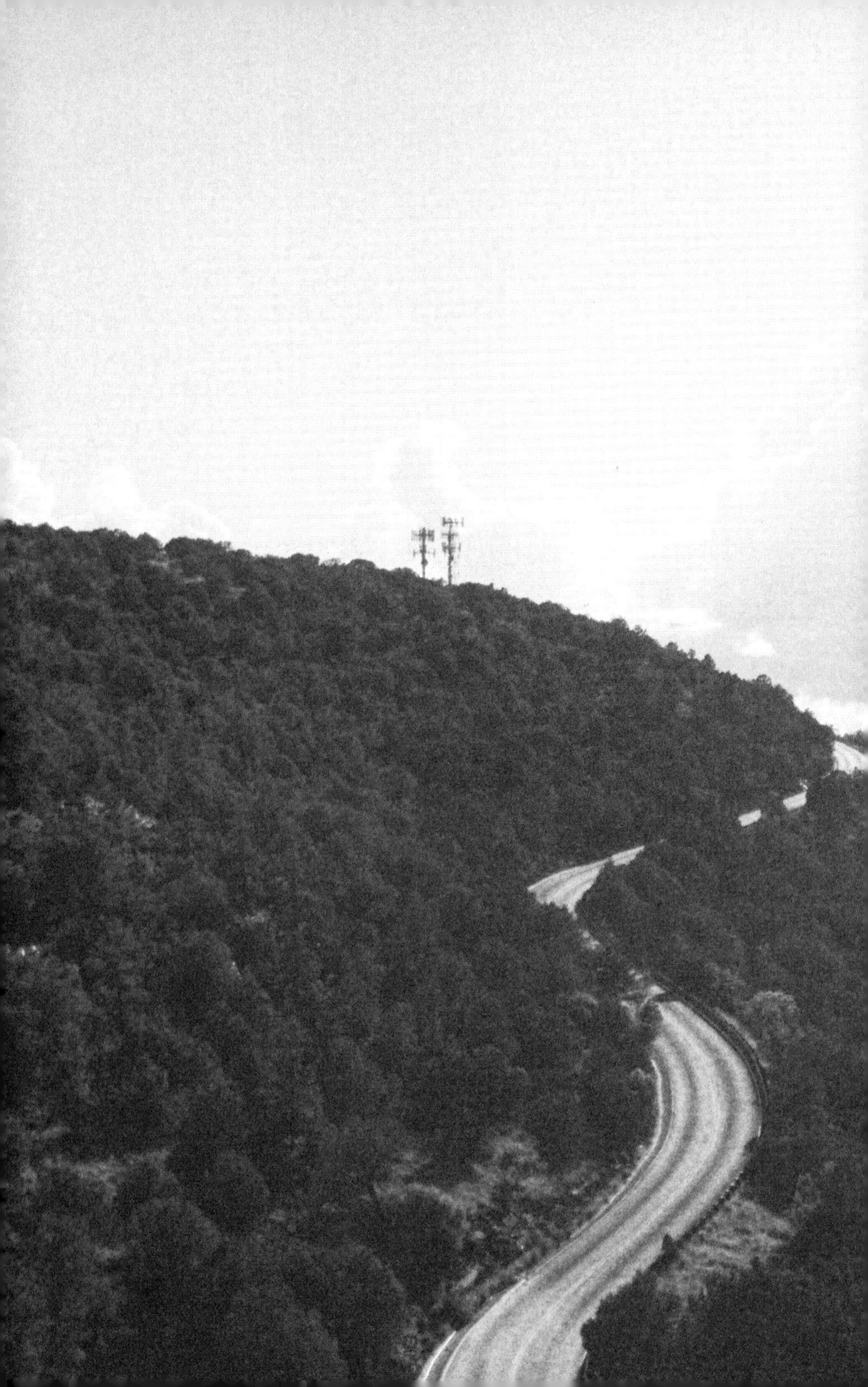

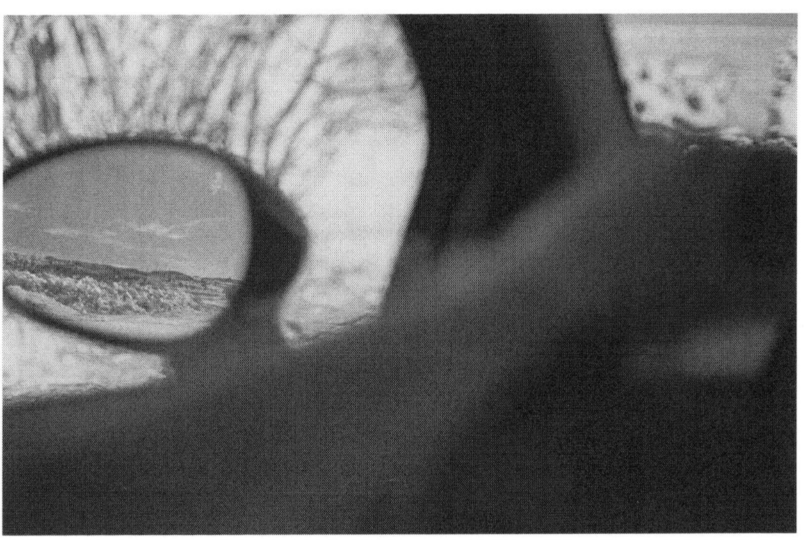

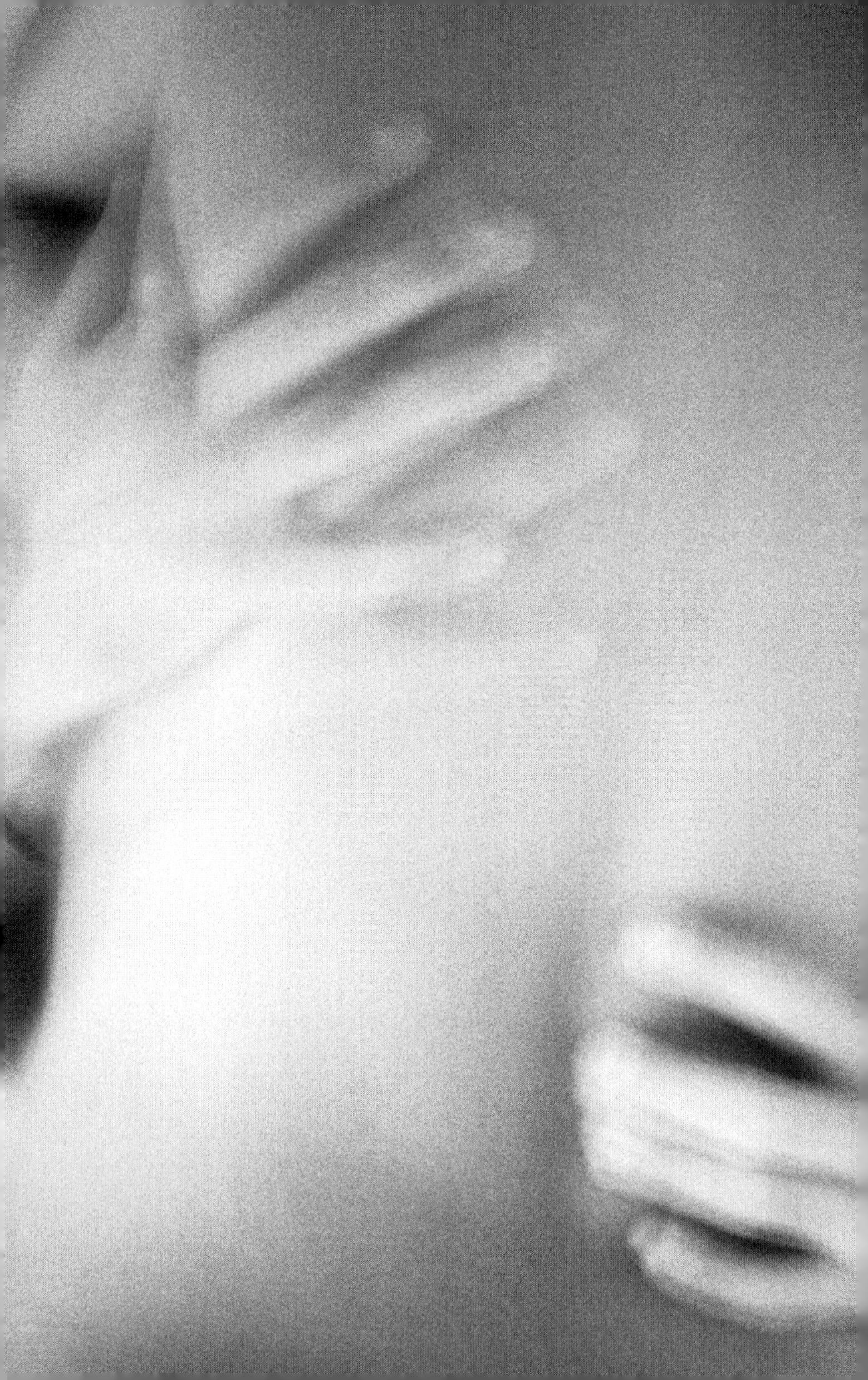

When I get to Austin, I'm surrounded by the ashes of people I've left for good or the embers of people I'm returning to. There's music and traffic in the air, and the smell of beer wafts up from the street.

I land for a couple of nights at Jeff's and replay our history in my head. I lay my head on his chest and say that I love him, because that's what I know I'm supposed to feel after we sleep together. And I'm supposed to feel it so much that I actually do feel it, even though he's done nothing but say stupid and angry things, smoke a lot of dope and ask me for a blowjob. The inequality of genders is so obvious these days I can only laugh instead of cry, because the place excluded from progress is desire. Tomorrow night he'll have some other girl seducing him with a cooked dinner, saying, "Don't worry, I don't even want a relationship, I'm not that kind of girl" or feeding the same romantic lie I'm living when I say "I love you." We lie in bed and I tell him the greatest heist ever perpetuated against women was convincing them that fucking is an act of their liberation. He strokes my bare back and calls it even.

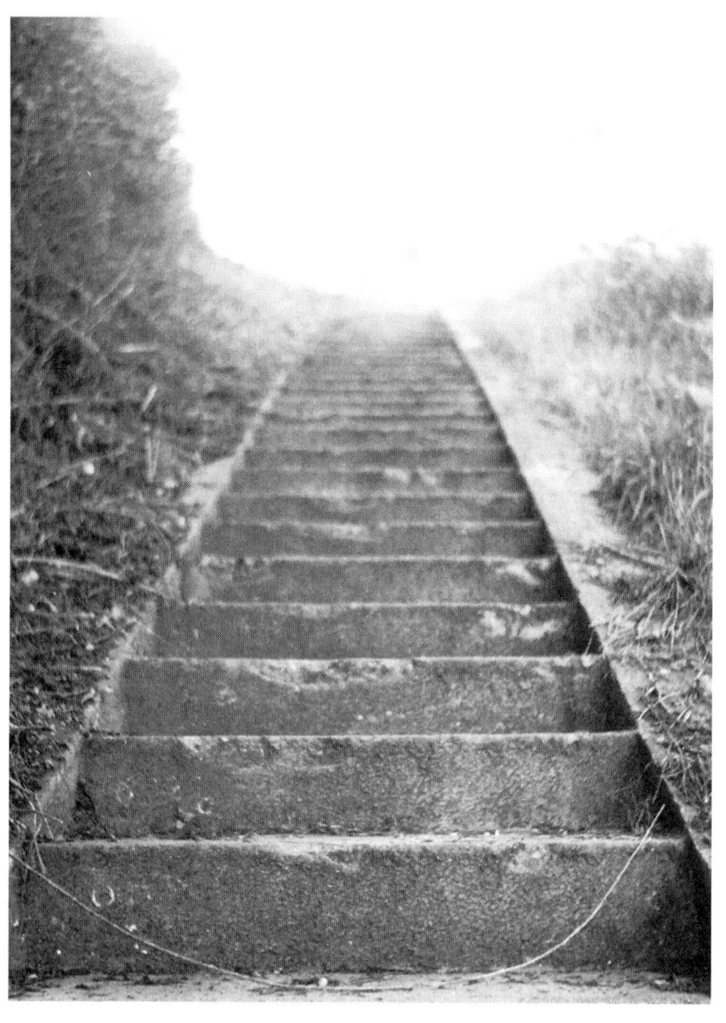

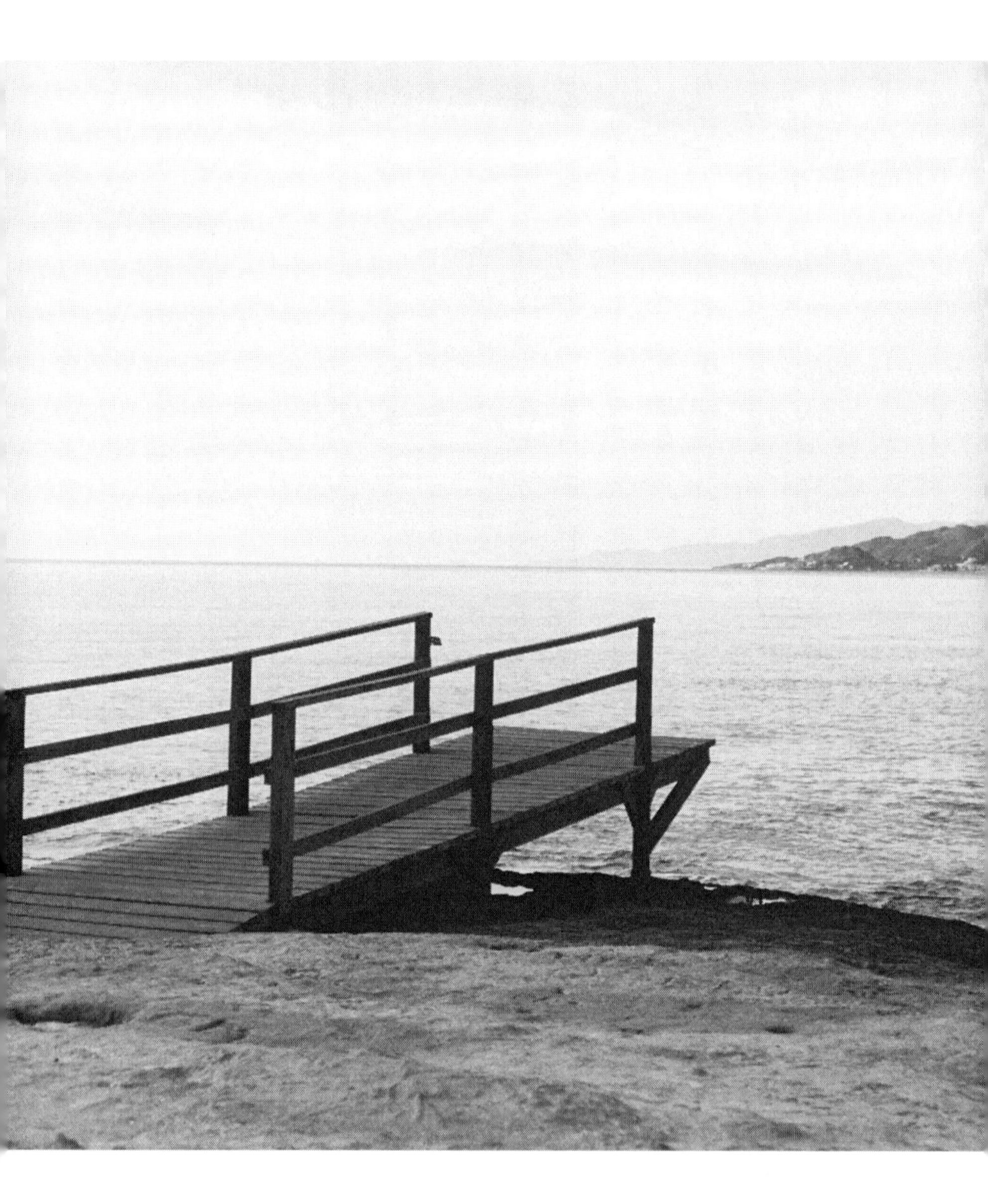

An old man calls over

to where I'm sitting on a bench, from around thirty paces away, and asks if I feel like talking. It's a reasonable enough request – I'm not doing anything but watching the water from up on a hill – though his proposition is made somewhat more ambiguous by the fact that he's completely naked.

His nakedness is not a problem in and of itself since I am, after all, at Hippie Hollow, a nudist lakeside beach in Austin, but we are the only two people present on this particular day (which makes complete sense considering it is winter and also raining) and I am not nude. I'm confounded for an explanation to give to him, or even myself, as to what I am doing at Hippie Hollow under these conditions except to say the following: I've been traveling around Texas, the state of my birth, for the last three weeks to work on a personal documentary project. I'm here to take pictures.

Naturally, one of the first things I start to consider, as his hairy wrinkled chest and hairless smooth legs take a seat next to me, is whether he would eventually allow me to take his picture. Being a woman, however, I automatically run several scenarios of personal safety through my mind. Gauging him for potential violence or psychosis, sizing up his possible strength in overpowering or outrunning me, I decide that he's relatively harmless and, in his completely naked state, carrying nothing but a small plastic cup, far more vulnerable than I am. And yet, despite this, I'm peripherally aware that this process of threat evaluation continues throughout our conversation. What I do not see coming is the monologue that emerges when I return his question and ask, "And what about you? Why are you here?"

The old man has a slowness to him, not necessarily one of age but of temperament. He's calm and unassuming, unaffected by the drizzling rain, his bare feet at home among the grass, rocks and roots that cover the hilly terrain. "Well," he begins slowly, the drawn-out introduction to a long story. "It's a long story."

"I am an angel," he continues in a clear voice, an urban Texan drawl. "But I am no different from a rock."

And he goes on to explain the philosophical absurdity of the cosmos and his nonsensical place within such chaotic stardust. Heaven is on Earth, just as the Earth is the heavens. All is equal, all is special. And equally, none of it is.

Now, I know a lot of people would write him off straight away, file him as crazy and make some excuse to leave or try to convince him of some more readily accessible reality. But with the beauty of time on my side, I stay. I listen.

And listen. For around two hours, as the sunset begins to fall over Lake Travis, I listen as he unleashes. He calmly rants madness, but I don't think he's crazy. He's just proffering an unvarnished version of every dark corner of his mind to see if I show signs of recognition. Am I the sort of person, he seems to pose, who will admit that my mind has dark corners, too?

"I didn't know if I would find anyone here today," he says, wiping the tears from his eyes with the heel of his hand. "Some people tell me I need help. They say, 'You need to go talk to someone.'" He exhales the inhumanity of this irony, long and mournful.

The more he speaks, the more he seems to me like anybody, confused about their significance as a sentient being in a cold and infinite universe. Another person who's spent a lifetime collecting experiences, alive with emotions and energy, and filled with a boundless potential for creation, only to be met time and again with the confinement of being functionally evaluated and dismissed by others. Another flesh-based being who knows that beyond our blood we are pure light—and nobody cares.

And part of the laughable disconnected farce of it all is that, in the background, I still wonder if that's what this encounter is really about. Does he really just need someone to talk to, or is this at some point going to become about something else? Sex, for example. My mind keeps returning to that if only because it's just him and me alone by a lake, and he's already naked.

At some point, I arrive at an internal decision, should he bring some invitation of sex into the dialogue: No, I am not willing to participate, but if he wanted to jerk off I'd be willing to watch.

It never comes up though, of course. Perhaps, just as I'm running questions about his intentions through my mind, he's doing the same: Is she really willing to just listen, or is it about something else?

An hour or so into the conversation, I ask if I can take his photo, and he answers by ignoring the question, talking about something else entirely. I'm not an asshole, I don't try to sneak a shot while he's distracted, but eventually, as another hour passes, because I am here to take photographs, I take out my camera and capture the view over the water instead.

The mood shifts. Now that my camera is in hand, he takes his leave.

I walk in the drizzle back to my rental car deliberating fair trades.

I leave with a portrait of a sunset instead of a person, but it was still a trade. I'd like to think that he walked away from that bench on the hill feeling richer, though I'll never know for sure. I walked away with a conversation in my head, the reward of having shut up long enough to hear someone else's story.

If I wasn't a photographer, would I go to a nudist beach on a rainy day in winter? If I wasn't a writer, would I be open to hearing the sad stories of a stranger? Is it the other way around? If I didn't do these things, would I feel alive at all?

I drive to the next place, some hipster café in the city that seems so far removed from a quiet conversation on a bench that when I arrive it feels like I've been on a long journey. I order a coffee from a barista with a fake smile delivered genuinely, but that exchange is only commerce. It's consequential.

I muse on that old man, and I already have trouble remembering what he looked like. Sitting right next to a person it's hard to examine them closely. The picture that I wanted to take can't quite hold still in my memory, its reality warps and dissipates like Fata Morgana. But I do not need the photo to document what I saw; the two of us spoke without owing each other anything.

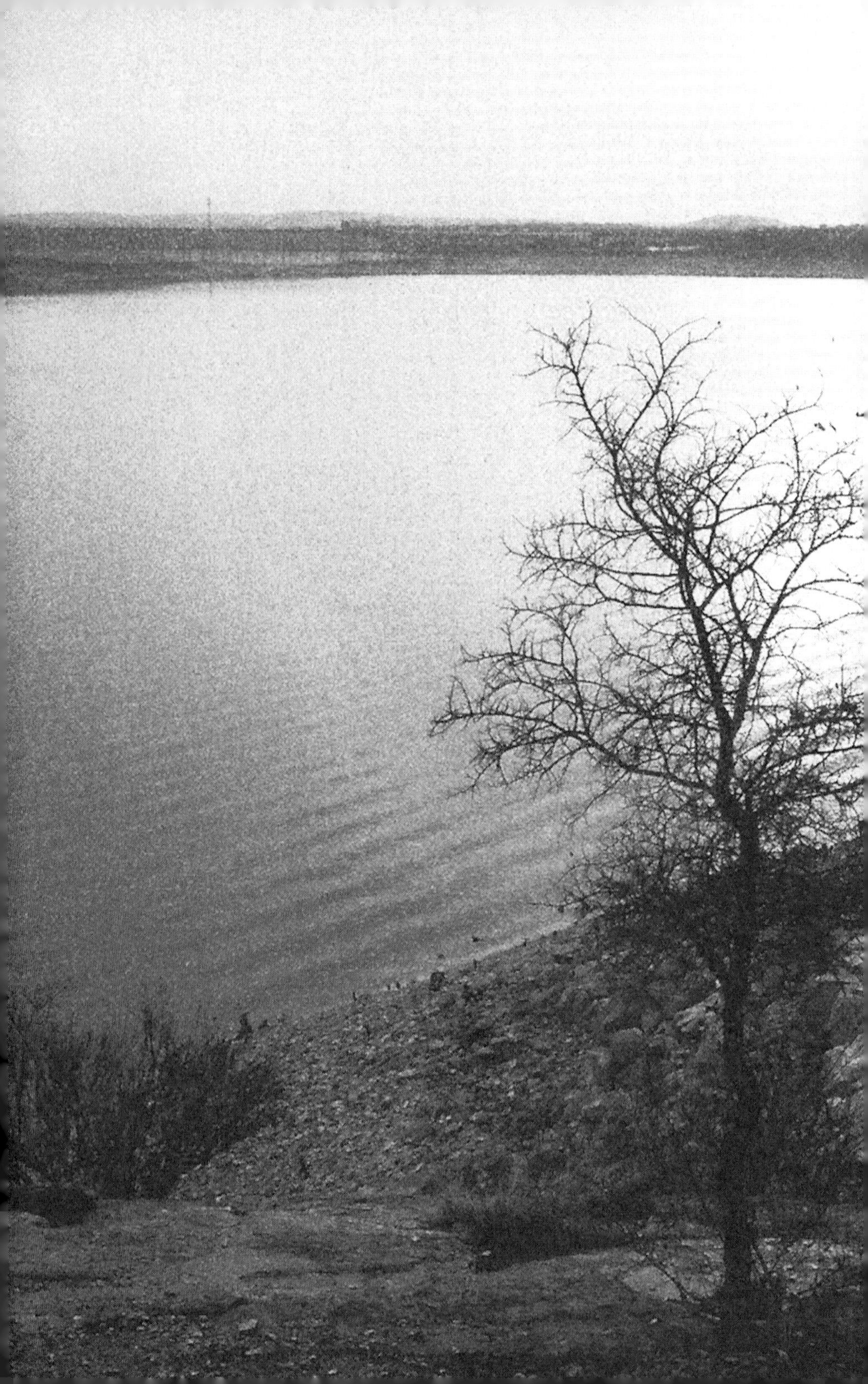

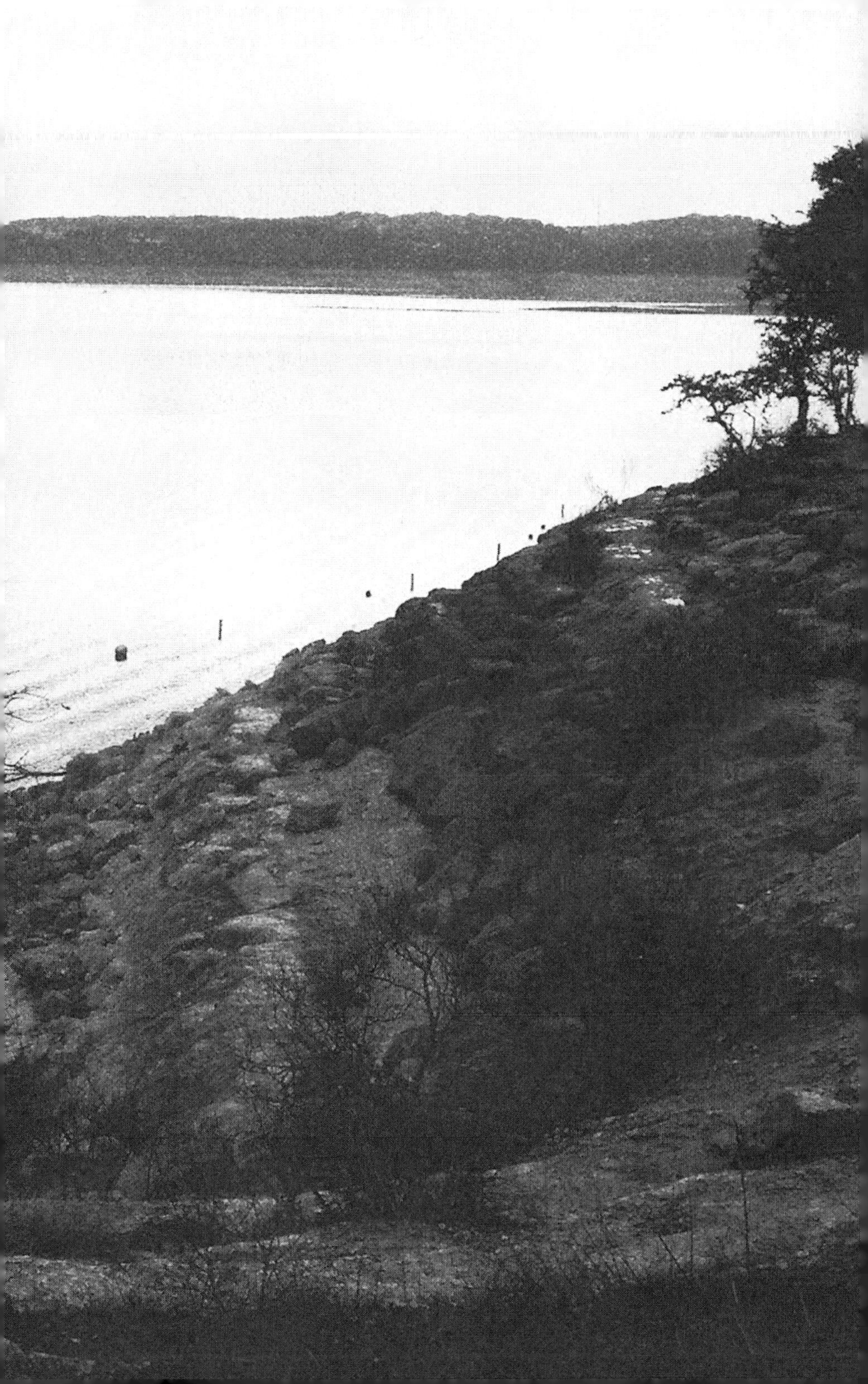

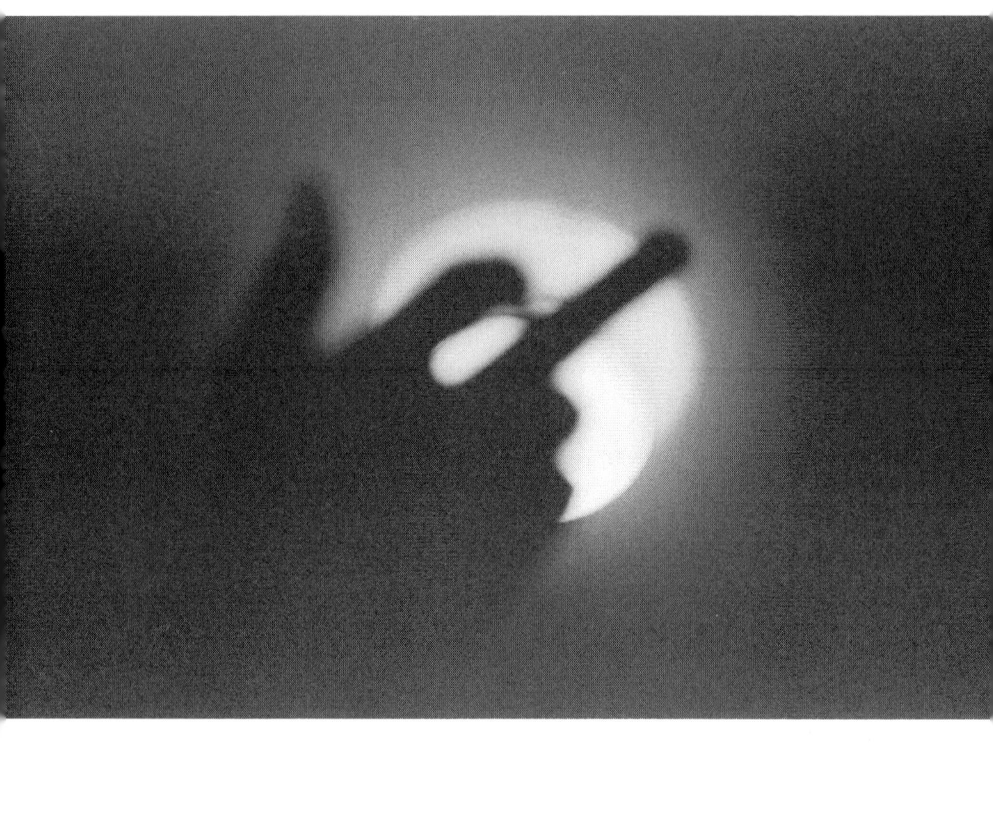

"I'm NOT going to write any more 'LOVE' STORIES,"

I said, emphasizing my contempt with fingers held high in quotation marks that stabbed the air like a striking rattlesnake.

"I didn't know you wrote love stories," Jeff said, falling back onto the sheets and discarding the used condom onto the hardwood floor with a moist thwack. "Oh, sorry, I mean 'love' stories."

"Maybe I never actually wrote them down, but I'm constantly writing them with my head," I said, pulling the sheets up around me in the absence of his body heat. "Little ridiculous romantifications of real life. Maybe that's why, by the time it could end up as words on paper, it's turned to ash."

We didn't kiss after the fact, or even all that much during. Kissing is for lovers. Neither of us had any delusions about what this was. Or, to be honest,

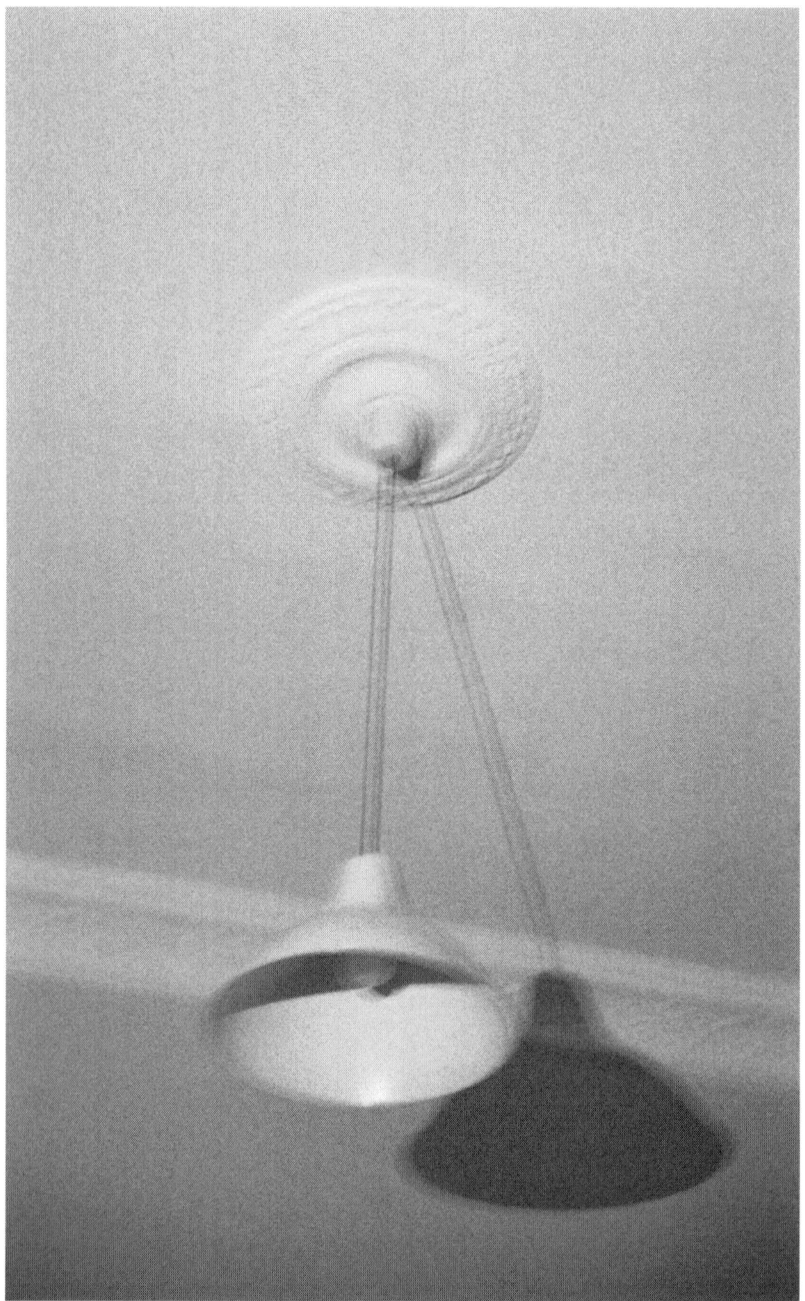

I had my delusions, but they were somewhere safely in middle-earth. On the surface, I knew it was nothing. Somewhere below that I thought it was something more, but deep down I knew it was nothing.

I kept waiting for Jeff to stop being the sexiest man I'd ever known, but more than fifteen years had gone by since the first time we'd slept together, and his looks aged along with him. Trying to break it down into parts, they were all clichés: tall and lean; a strong jawline; a dark, full head of hair; deep blue eyes that changed color according to what he was wearing; sharp white teeth and a mischievous smile. These days, his eyes were often glazed and watery with dope, and that was probably his one saving grace of physical imperfection, but in the dark as we were, I could just see the line of his profile as he lay in the sheets catching his breath.

With my head by the edge of the bed, I could see the balled-up wad of latex, and I was glad it wasn't my floor. I've always thought you can tell a lot about a man by what he does with the condom afterward—some wadding it into a tissue, some flushing it down a toilet, some tying it into a neat knot with substance saved, and some merely tossing it onto the floor like a cigarette butt. I'm sure there is something to be learned by this characteristic act of disposal, but I haven't yet figured out what.

With Jeff now, I suspected he was too exhausted to give a fuck about anything at all. That was the overall impression I'd gotten from him the last couple of days I'd been sleeping on his couch.

"Love stories fill our heads with such lies," I said, and Jeff nodded, not giving a fuck.

Tired as he was, he was asleep in no time at all, and I lay in the dark watching the street light cast onto the ceiling through venetian blinds—a series of long, yellow strips. I was grateful to him because he always knew how to break my heart gently. Maybe that's the most you can ask of anybody.

Nora and I were going to leave the next day, and in my desperation to belong anywhere, to anyone, I wished he would ask me to stay. I knew he wouldn't, and even if he did we'd kill each other shortly. I pulled myself up against his body, smelled his shoulder, kissed his skin to get a taste of his particular elixir. He was sweat and sawdust and motorcycle leathers. All the wanting in the world couldn't make it work.

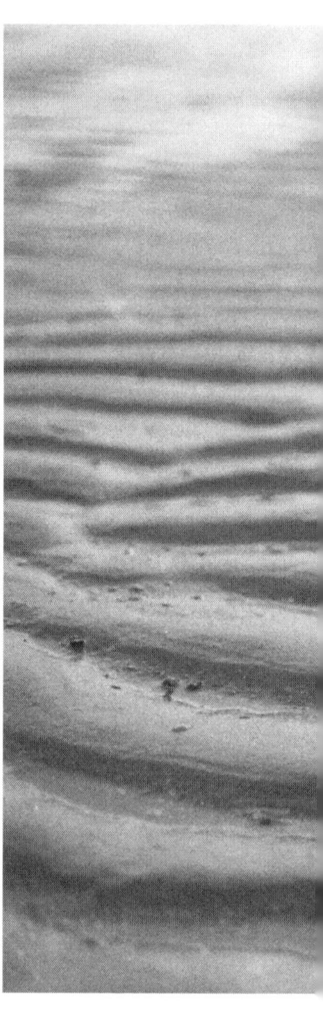

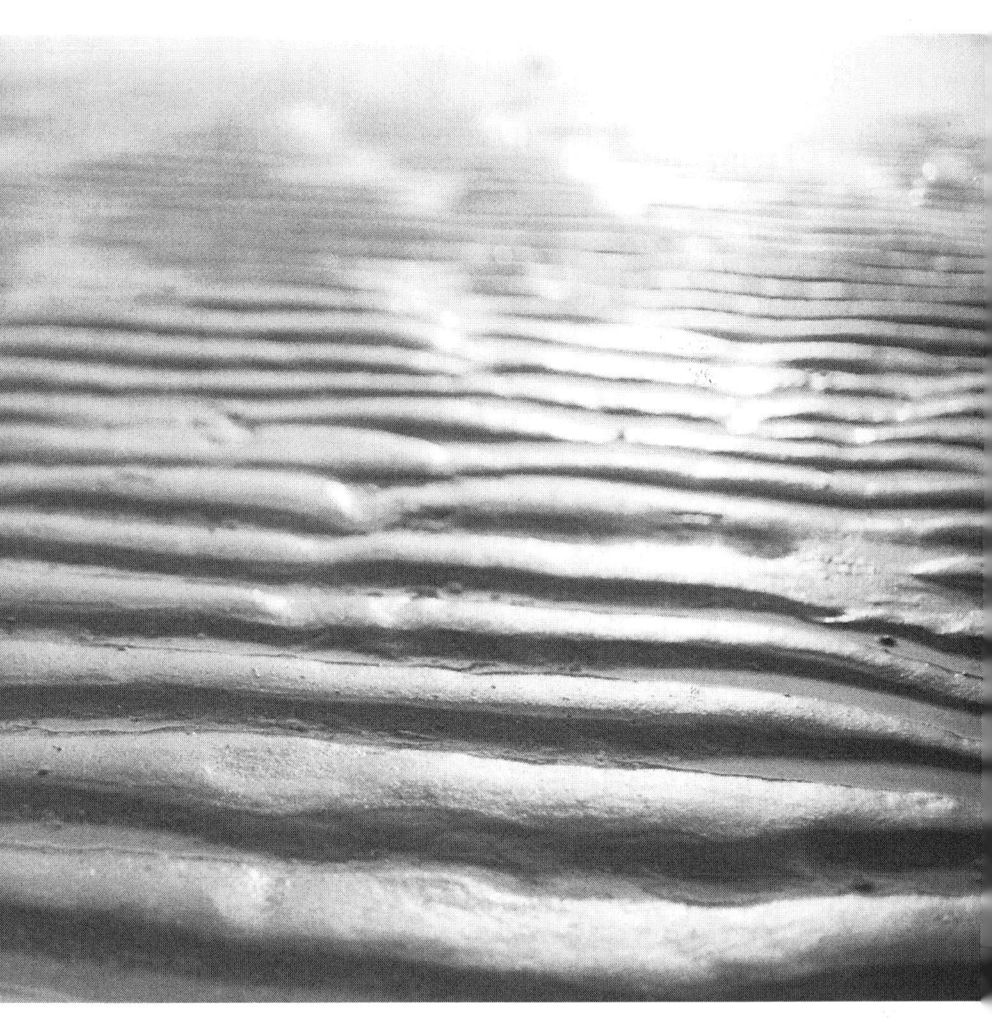

He got up early to go to work and gave me a ceremonial kiss goodbye, which I appreciated. I awoke much later in his plaid flannel sheets, feeling foreign among the things of his life and glad to go. I took a shower in the bathroom that wasn't mine, made coffee in the kitchen that wasn't mine, and sat on the back porch in the summer shade to drink it—another place I loved, kind of, but that wasn't mine.

I packed my bag and surveyed the house for anything I might have forgotten. The small bathroom held a small stepladder to help his son reach the sink, and I folded it and set it against the wall. Two toothbrushes, one shorter and fatter than the other and adorned with a cartoon monster, stood in a cup whitened by dried toothpaste. I washed the cup as best I could to remove the residue and wiped down the sink. A few steps away in the living room/dining room combo, I straightened the papers and toys that lay around the dining table and refolded the blanket across the back of the couch. I ran my fingers carefully along the teeth of a giant rusty saw that hung above the couch, a decoration that only a handyman living alone could love.

My suitcase, bruised by countless planes and trains but somehow still fancier than anything in the house, sat next to the door distinctly out of place. I felt embarrassed but assured, like a fraud who'd finally become the thing she was faking.

An old Southern admonishment ran through my head: *You're gettin' too big for your britches.*

It was good to leave, it was the right thing. But it still serrated into me, the sharp divide between the person I was and one of the lives I could have been living and wasn't.

I start the car and Nora asks me if I'm okay and I say no, as though it's about him. It's not, and I know it's not, but I'm shaking anyway. It's about a lifetime of disillusionment consummated one twenty-minute dose at a time.

These are the times we live in: the casual sex institutionalized complex. The mass-ingested half-boredom of fucking because you can and because it's the closest thing to intimacy that you can fake without revealing anything about yourself other than your skin.

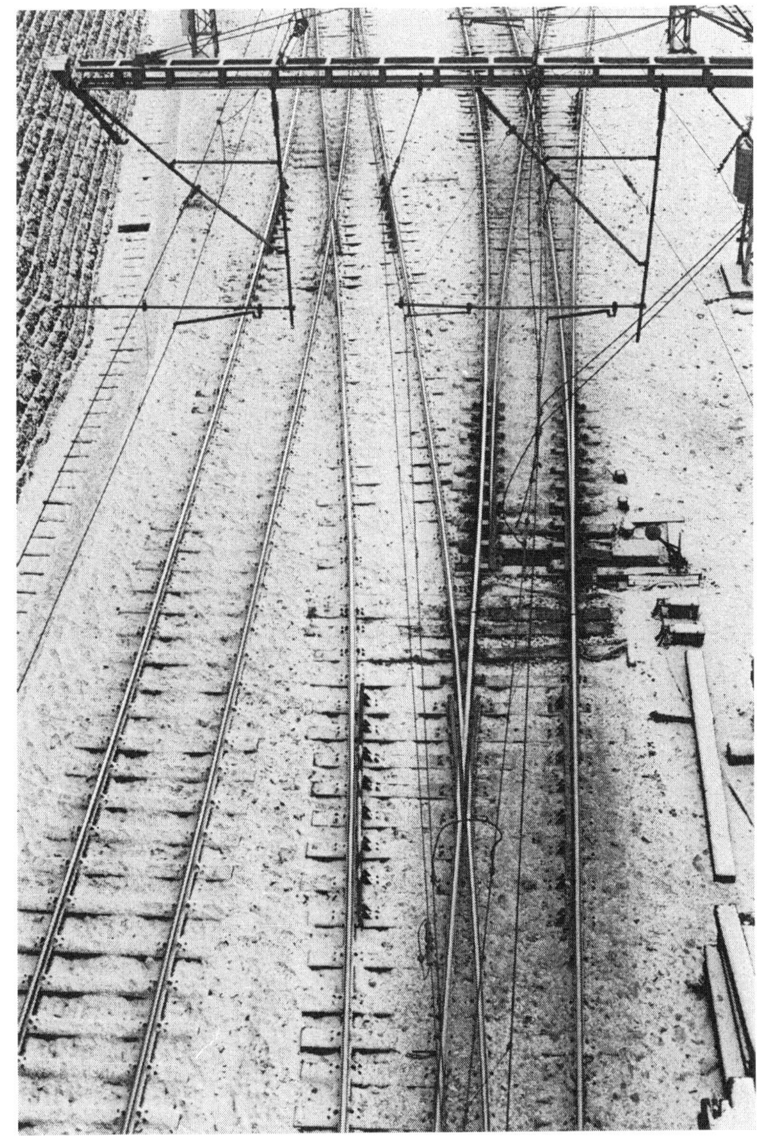

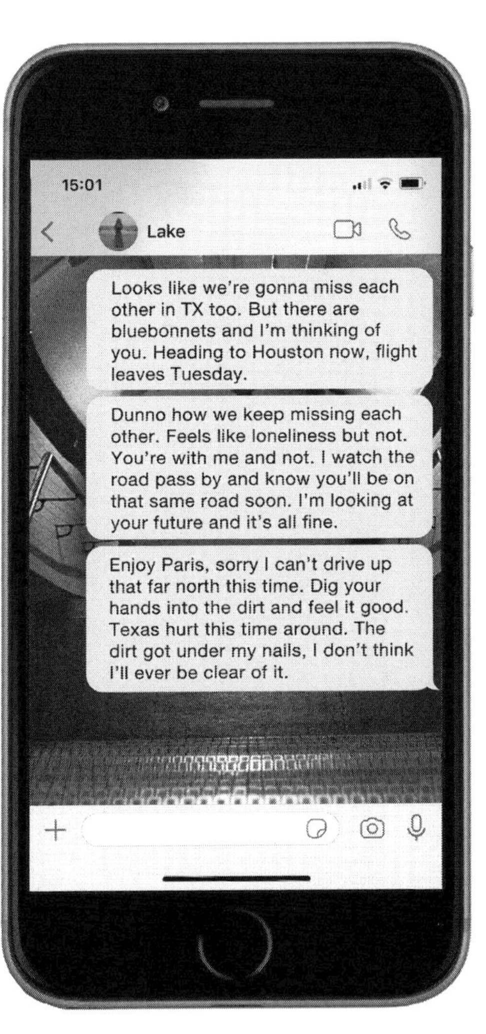
15:01
Lake
Looks like we're gonna miss each other in TX too. But there are bluebonnets and I'm thinking of you. Heading to Houston now, flight leaves Tuesday.
Dunno how we keep missing each other. Feels like loneliness but not. You're with me and not. I watch the road pass by and know you'll be on that same road soon. I'm looking at your future and it's all fine.
Enjoy Paris, sorry I can't drive up that far north this time. Dig your hands into the dirt and feel it good. Texas hurt this time around. The dirt got under my nails, I don't think I'll ever be clear of it.

My laundry is drying. A cat is sleeping on my chest as I lie on the couch watching the rain. The rain again.

It all moves so slowly, though I'm not sure where the weeks have gone this year. The colors of autumn in Amsterdam are yellow dying and grey empty. I try to fall asleep, wishing for the day to go faster so that I might wake up tomorrow to something better. I don't know why some days are so determined to be beyond my grasp. I always think that in my next life I'll be a person who will be able to appreciate the spread of time and marvel in every minute of counting raindrops because I know it's the right thing to do, that it's the way to show gratitude for being alive. But in only one lifetime I can't learn to do everything right. There have been so many days that came and went while I was wishing.

My sister hugs me goodbye, and says with a kind of laugh, "Well... See you next year, I guess."

And I cannot say anything while my heart is breaking.

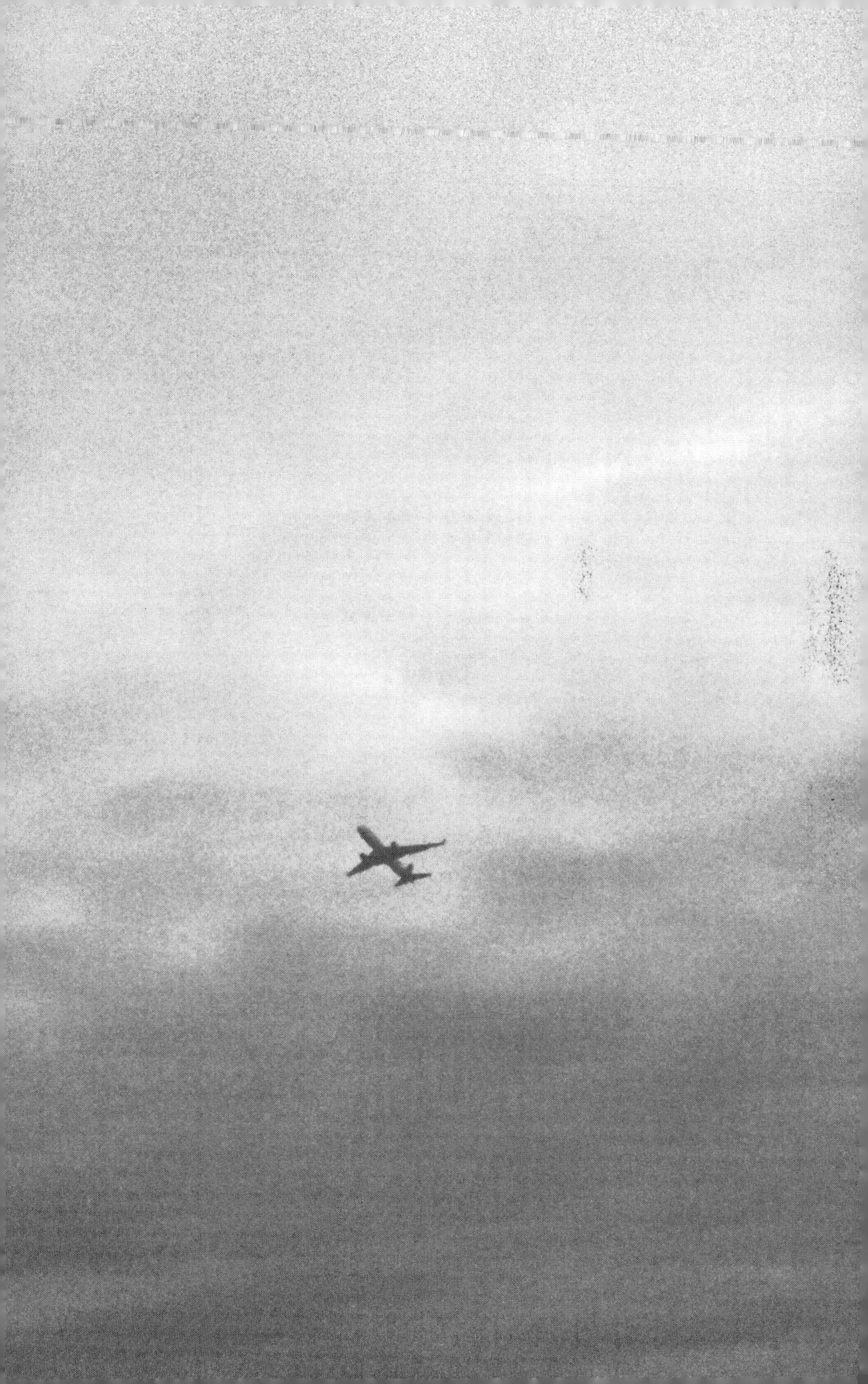

I am a
SICK WOMAN,

I am an

UNPLEASANT WOMAN,

I think **my heart** is DISEASED.

I land in Valencia for the third time in six months, some twisted mix of business and pleasure, flavors swirled together like a sundae cone.

I drive south solo through the desert and hills, revving the engine of a miniature rental car with a laugh. Hugging the road's curves, I sing along to the tinned-can sound of the car stereo.

The Spanish sun
shines through the car
windows, and I exit from the
highway at a random town because
I can.

I sit and have a café con leche
and then get back in my car and
drive some more.

I pull to the side of the road and
take a photograph of
a broken building
because I can, and then
get back in the car
and drive more.

I stop to look at
a particularly nice tree
because I can.

I choose where I go and
when I stop and each choice
feels like a strengthening of self.

I drive all day this way, and
it's not enough.

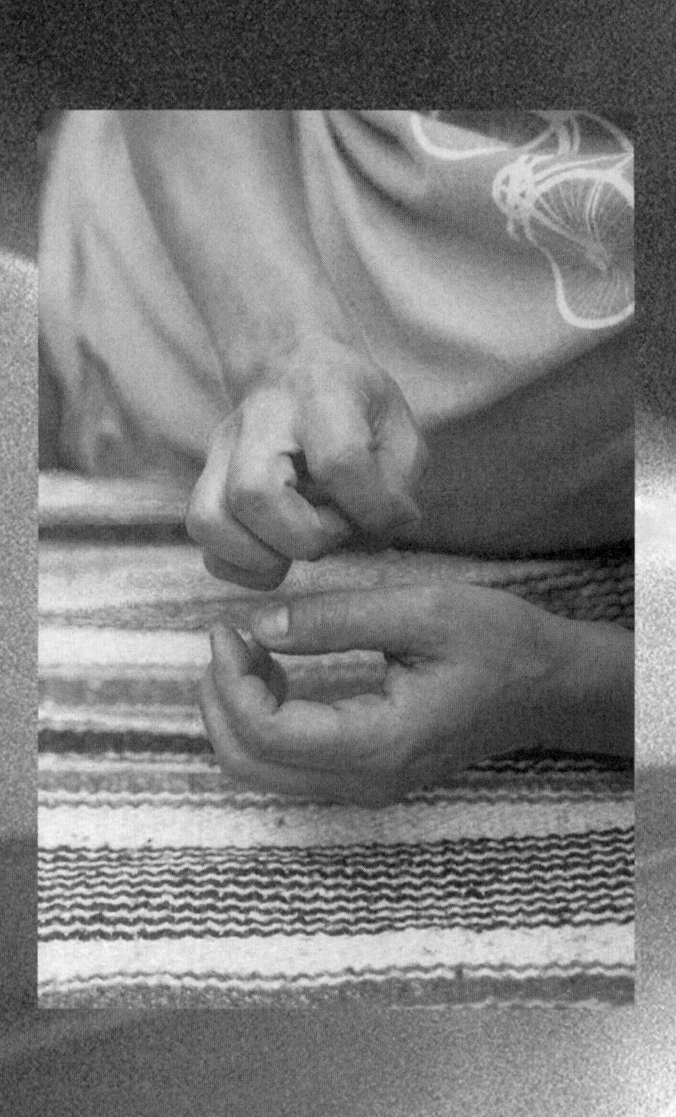

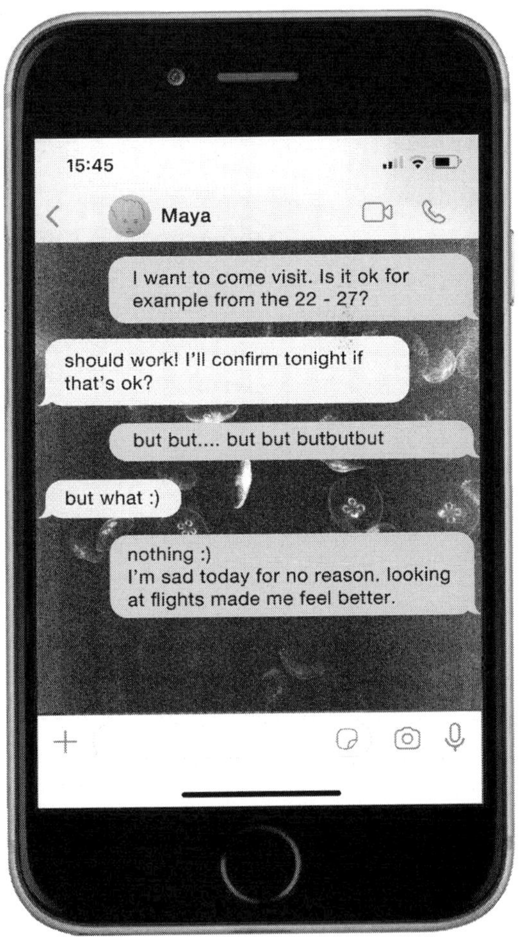

15:45
Maya
I want to come visit. Is it ok for example from the 22 - 27?
should work! I'll confirm tonight if that's ok?
but but.... but but butbutbut
but what :)
nothing :)
I'm sad today for no reason. looking at flights made me feel better.

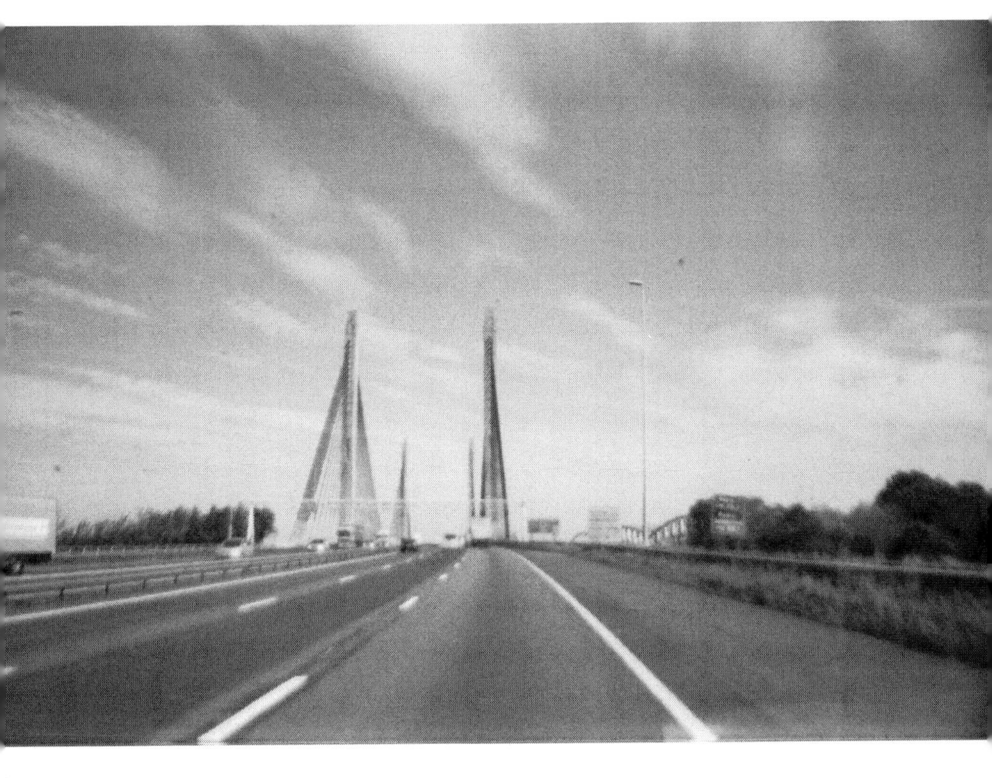

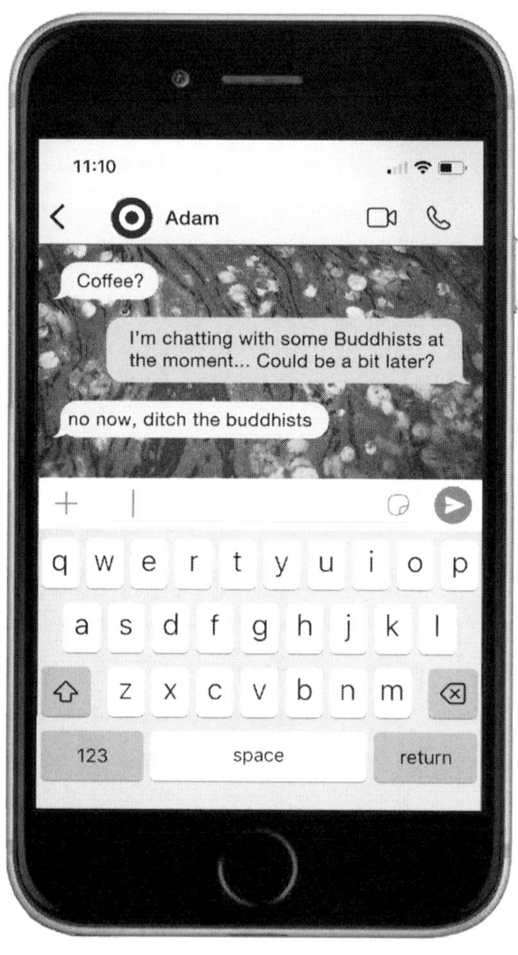

11:10
Adam
Coffee?
I'm chatting with some Buddhists at the moment... Could be a bit later?
no now, ditch the buddhists
q w e r t y u i o p
a s d f g h j k l
z x c v b n m
123 space return

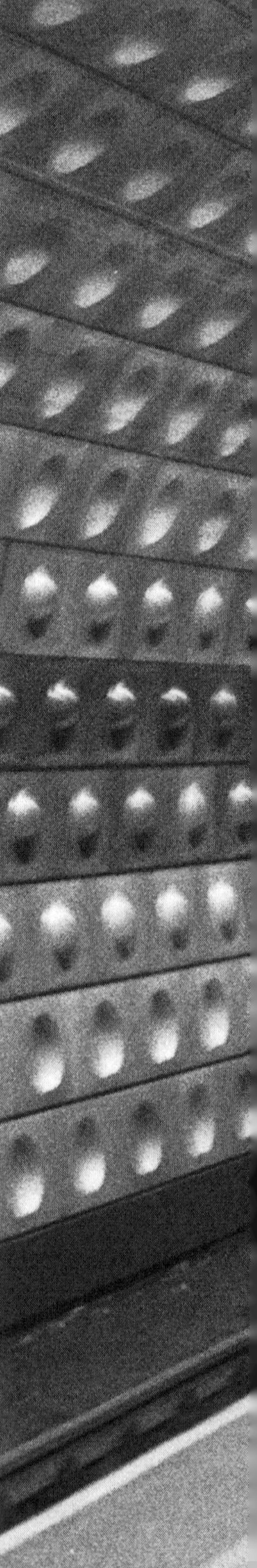

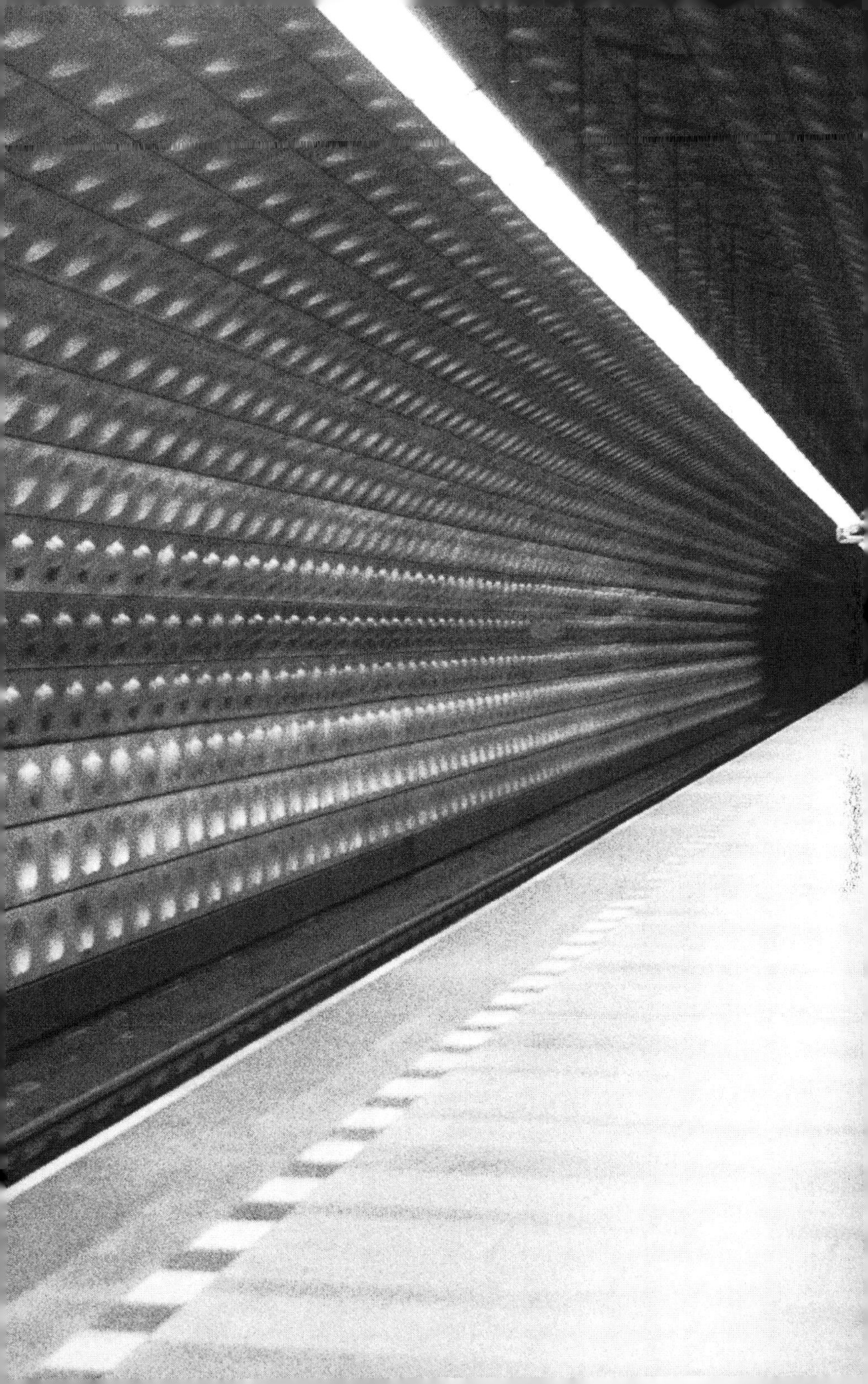

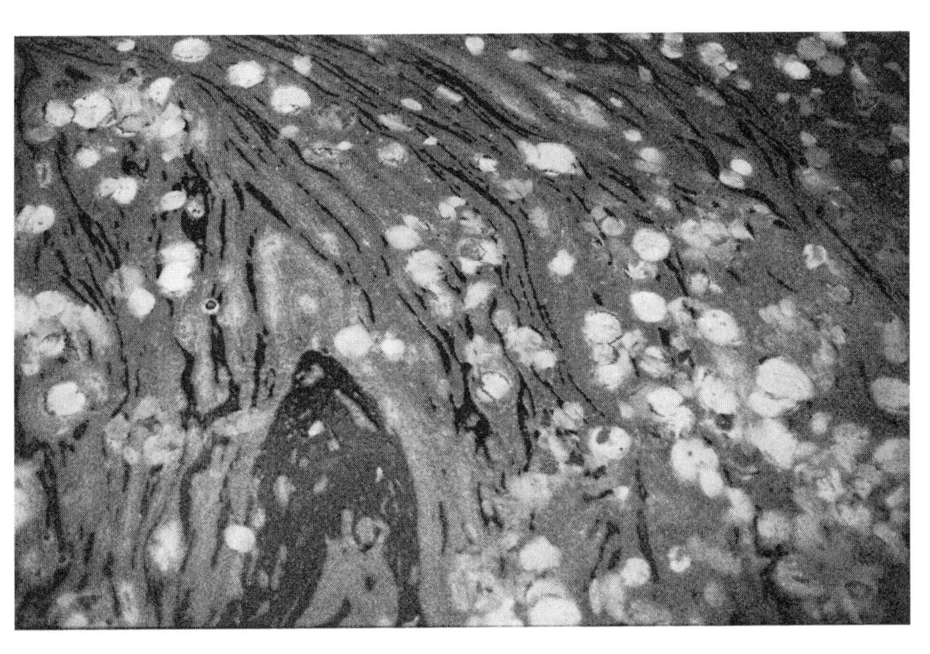

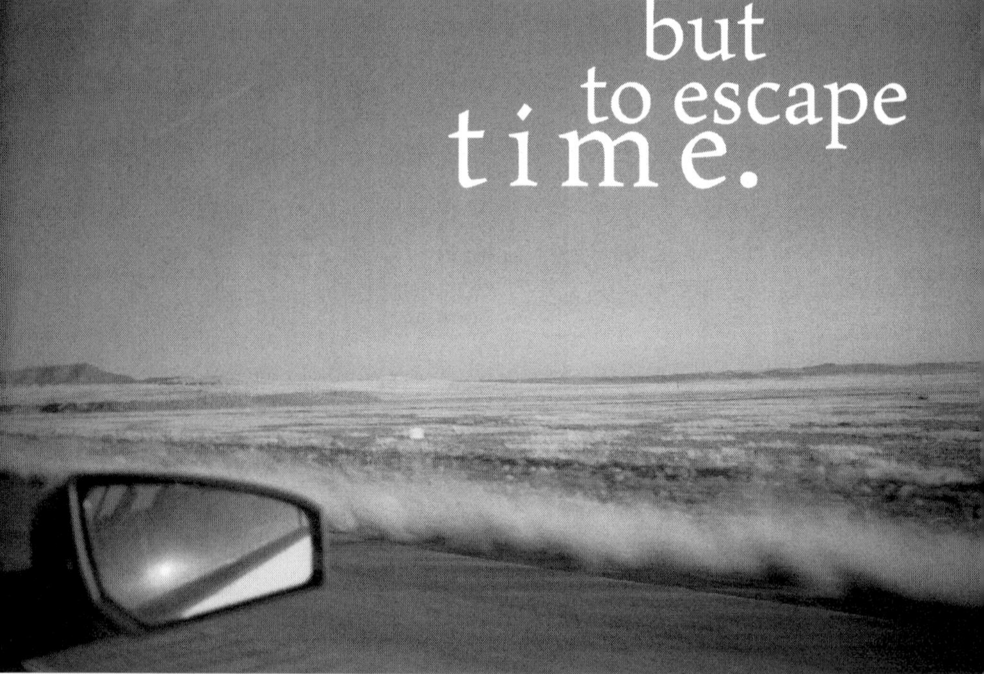

MAYBE
going elsewhere
was an effort
not to escape LOCATIONS
but
to escape
time.

In trying to keep moving I was keeping ahead of the current moment, skipping ahead of the now and ending up not "where" but "when."

Kerouac seemed to use travel as a means to escape accountability, his characters terminally unrepentant in their search for a self-reinforcing dharma. For me, movement was a kind of medicine, and when I slowed down long enough to take a hard look in the mirror, I was able to feel precisely when its effects wore off. If I stayed put, the link between cause and effect was inextricable. I don't know why some feel the weight of that with more force, with burdensome proportion. Missteps are in truth as common and inconsequential as raindrops, yet they ravaged me as storms. I wasn't aiming to escape accountability but rather the weight I bestowed it with. I had no expectation that the examined life – that only life worth living – would come freely or lightly, but I'd learned that its heaviness could be made lighter as I moved. To keep traction in a curve, accelerate.

There was no exception to the equation of action and reaction, and consequences always came due, but movement added sufficient noise that the formula could be upset. Distorted. Outcomes arrived, inevitably, but I could be spared the monstrosity of seeing them head-on.

Consequences look so much smaller in the rearview mirror.

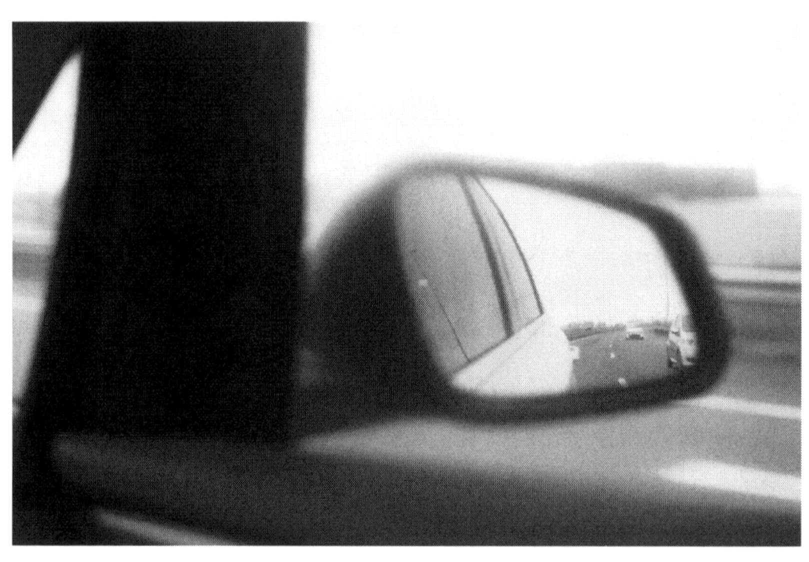

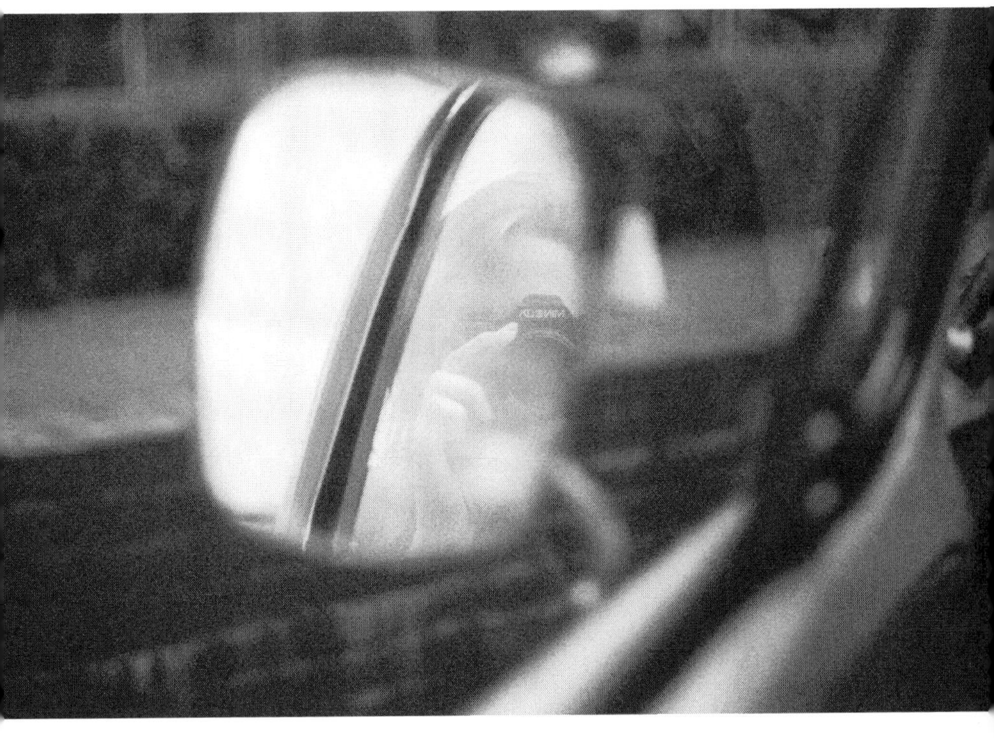

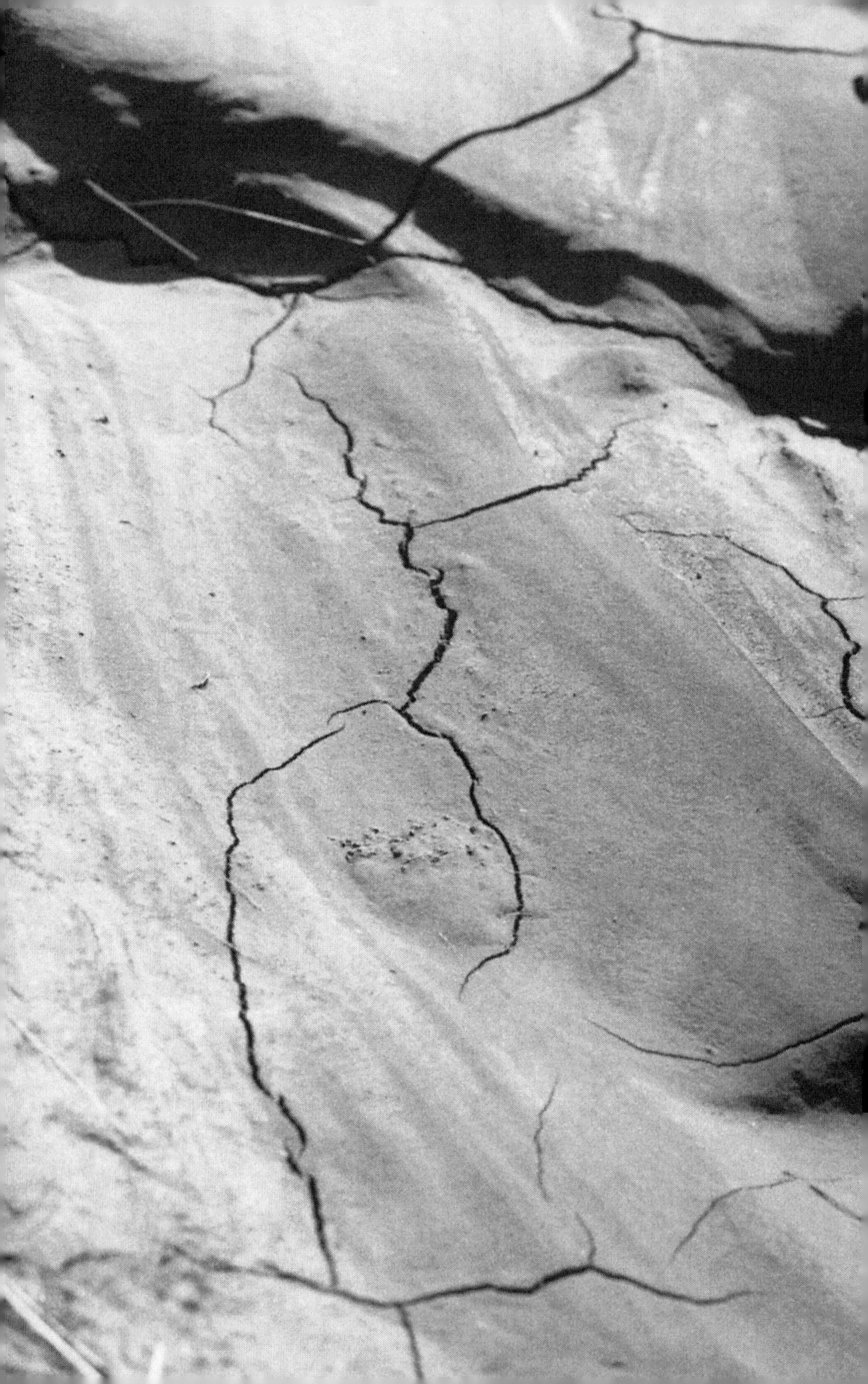

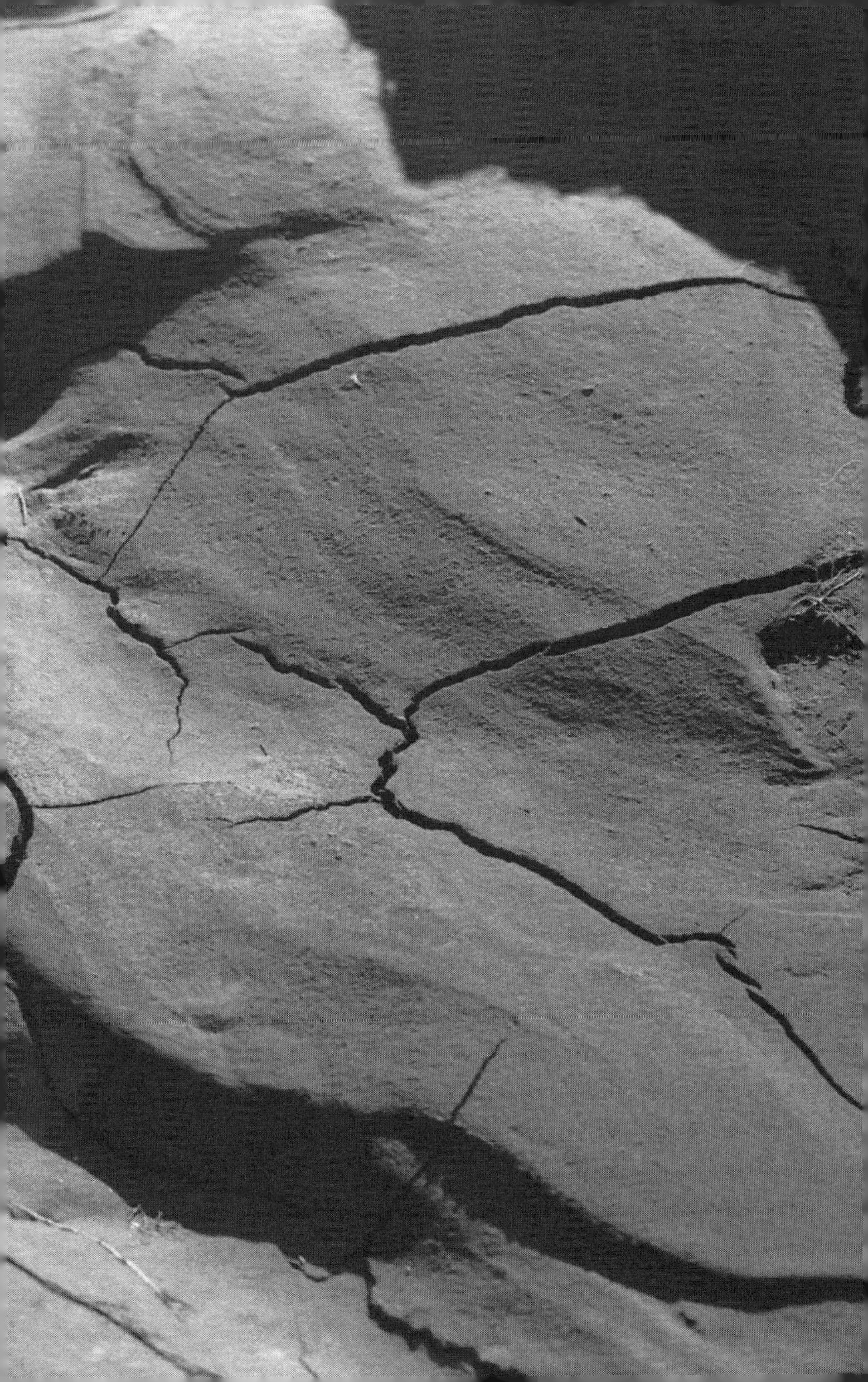

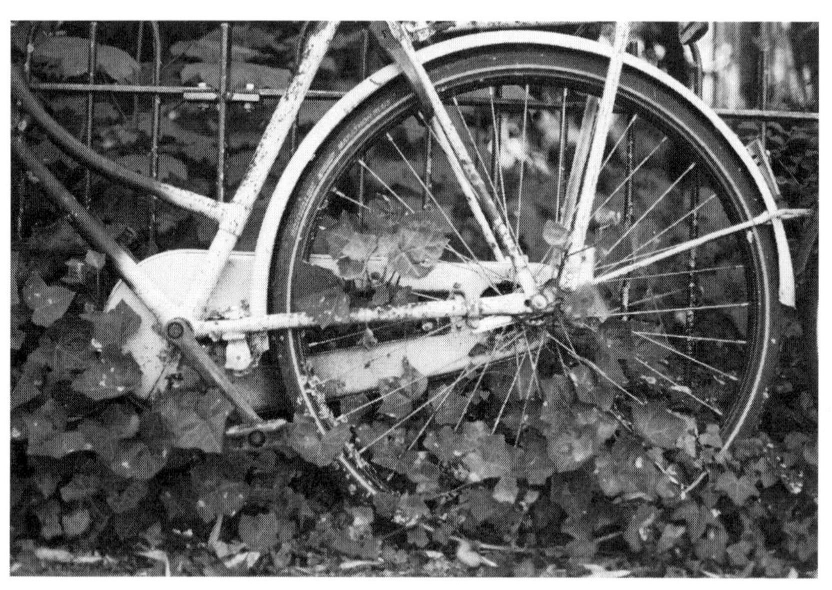

Koan reclined on my couch, tapping on his phone with one brain and watching TV with the other.

"Can't you stop that?" I ask, irritated beyond proportion for the thing that I should've just accepted about him by now but am still determined to see as something he can grow out of.

"Fine, Katherine. FINE!" he shouts, falling into character.

I want to know what happened to silence, what happened to stillness. And maybe it's all a joke because I'm no one to judge. I recite Blaise Pascal like scripture: *All of humanity's problems stem from the inability to sit quietly in a room alone.*

Koan tosses his phone down, but his hands don't know what to do; his eyes are bored by the room, the TV, me. He reclaims and fidgets with his phone even with the screen off.

He tells me: "I fucked the 18-year-old again."

I say, "Do you want an award?"

"Yeah, I do," he says. "Don't you know, Katherine? An 18-year-old is the cherry on the cake. You can't get any better."

He says these things to provoke me, I know. It's all part of the game but it still gets under my skin despite myself, and that's exactly why he says them.

He unlocks his phone again and starts texting with some girl; it didn't even matter who.

"Are you sleeping with anyone?" he asks.

"What for?" I retort, slipping into my own role like a pair of comfortable shoes.

"Maybe you should," he says.

"So I can feel alienated and alone and awful?"

"That's so fucked up!" he shouts, throwing his hands wildly into the air. "We have to fix this."

"Being different isn't fucked up, Koan."

"Come on, Moneypenny, let's go to a club and get you laid."

"I don't want to get laid, James. I know better. You don't have to understand."

"You think you're too smart to just fuck some really hot guy or even some really boring guy, but you might be wrong Kathnip. Come on, it might make you feel better."

"There's no evidence in support of that," I say.

"When was the last time?" he asks.

"At least a year," I say. "That half-French guy." And I watch Koan shudder with some thought unfathomable to him. He pities me, I know, but that's his business.

"You're like a priest or something," he says.

"Is that a bad thing? I'm living how I want to live."

"But you're so unhappy alone."

"Me and life get along just fine."

"Just fuck someone. Please."

"Would that make you feel better about my life? Seriously, the things you think are happiness are nothing like happiness for me."

"So what's happiness then? What am I doing wrong?"

"You're not doing anything wrong, Koan. You're living how you want to live. It's just not how I want to live. If it makes you happy to put your dick into anything resembling a living woman, fine. Do it. I figured out what works for me, so I'm doing that."

"What about that asshole you sent a love letter to. Do you regret writing him that idiotic letter?"

"Pff, no. You could wallpaper an IKEA with all the love letters I've written."

Koan laughed. "Good." He picks up his phone again, flips it a couple of times in his hand, then pounds it against his leg. "I just wish you wouldn't let these guys get to you. You're better than that."

"My life is very good, Koan. Maybe sometimes I wish I was somewhere else, or doing something else, or even that I had someone else around, but that's just life. I know what I'm doing."

"When we met, you were massively fucked up and depressed."

"And now I'm not."

"So you've got it all figured out now?"

"Maybe what I figured out is that the universe is my homegirl."

He's back to his phone, and I can't stand to watch the speed with which he texts various people, his phone constantly buzzing. Every time we get into it like this, I ask myself why we bother. It's surrogate for something, I know, but you could break down any relationship like that, everything coming down to some deep emptiness in our man-made lives, a god-shaped hole that we keep trying to fill with something else. But in many ways, what Koan and I did together was the most human thing in my life. We had learned how to exist together and still be alone.

Koan keeps his eyes on his phone and says: "That's so fucking stupid, Katherine."

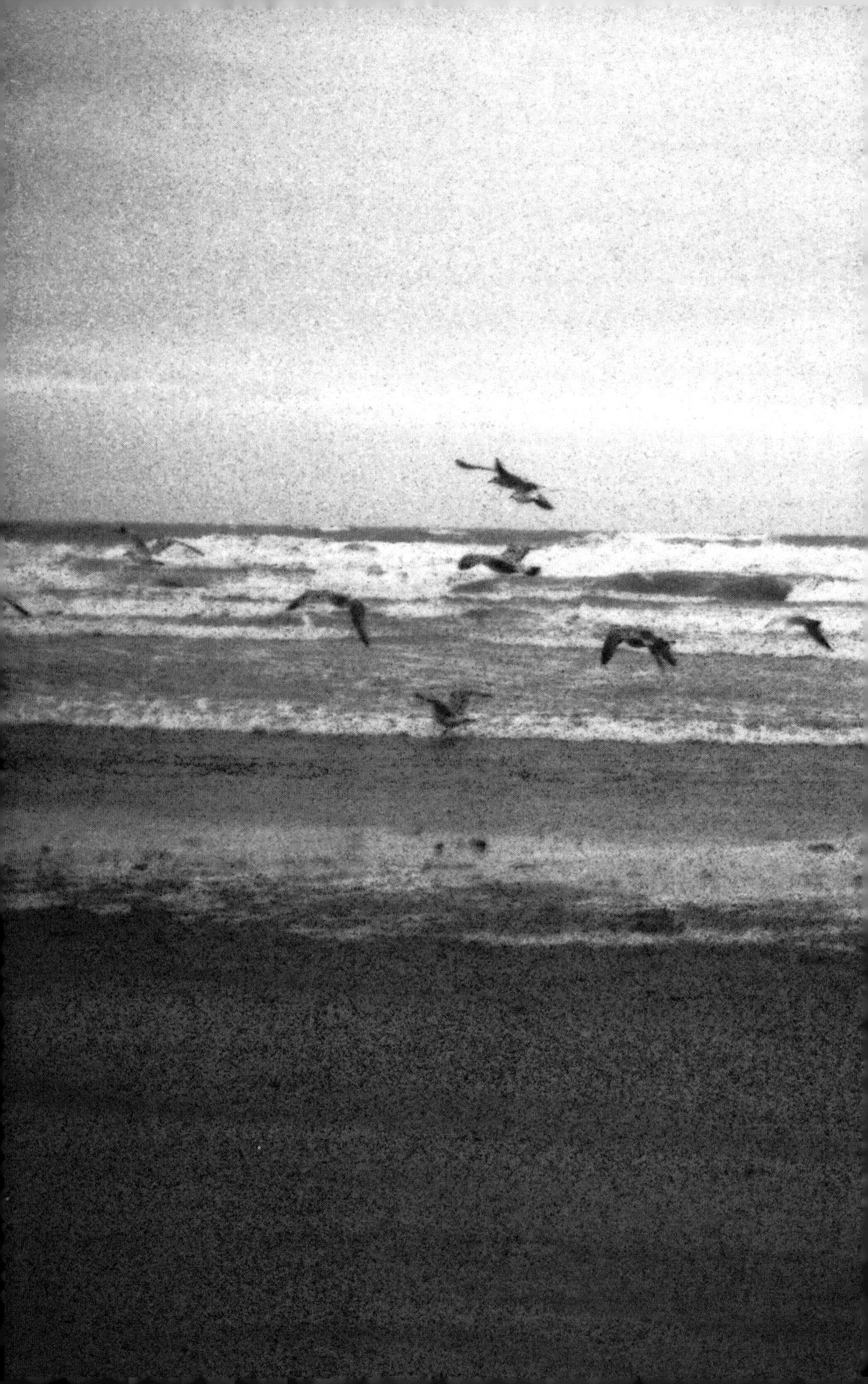

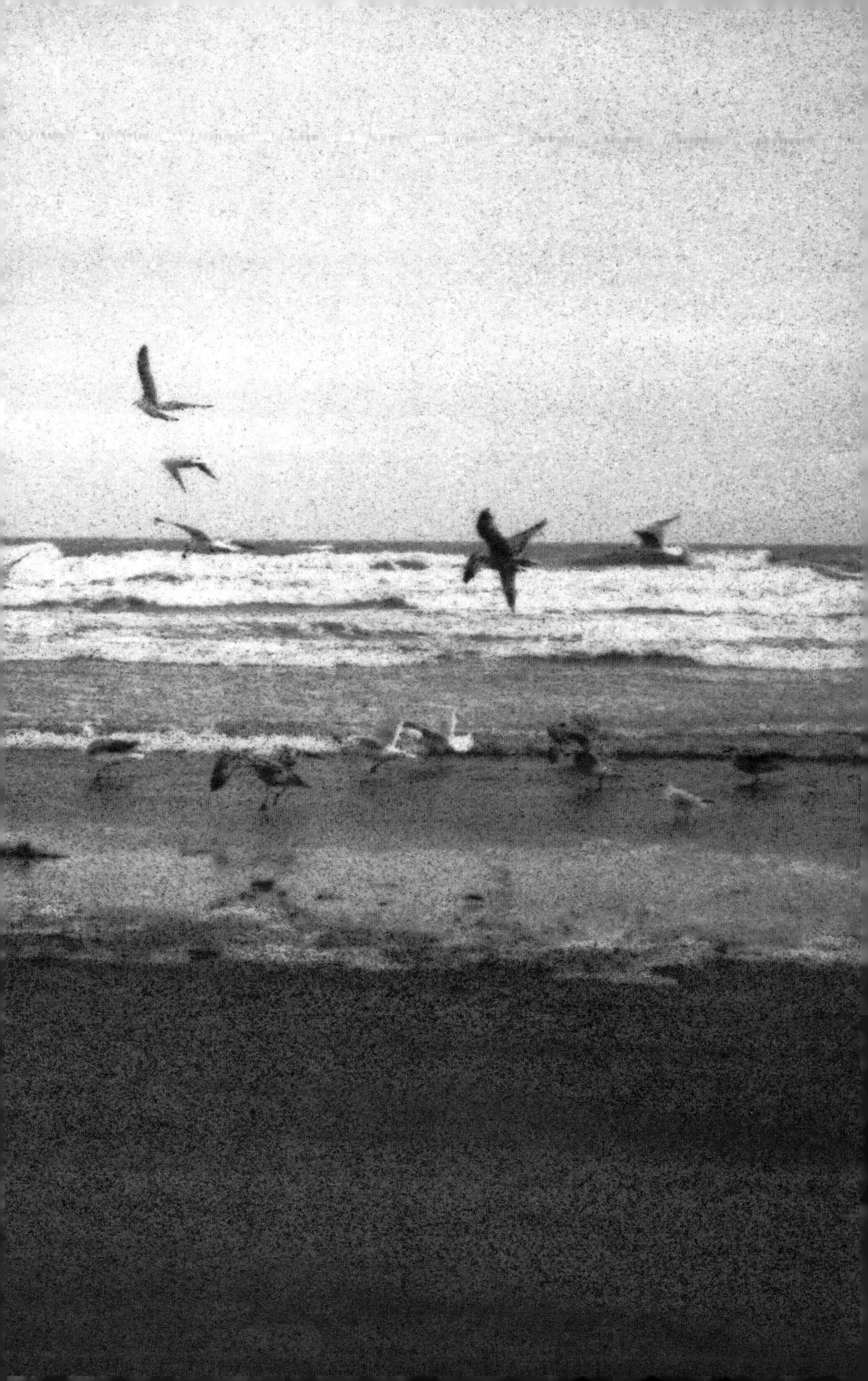

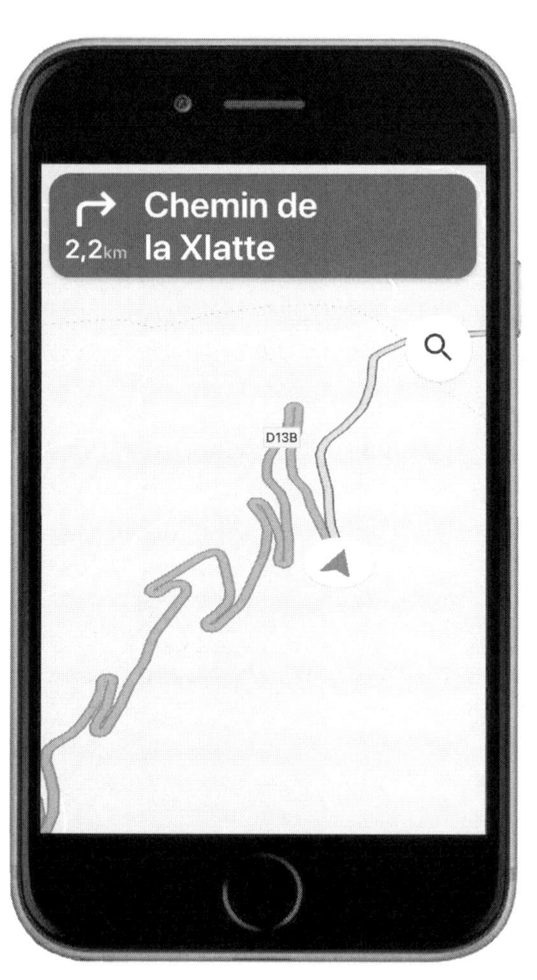

Chemin de
2,2km la Xlatte
D13B

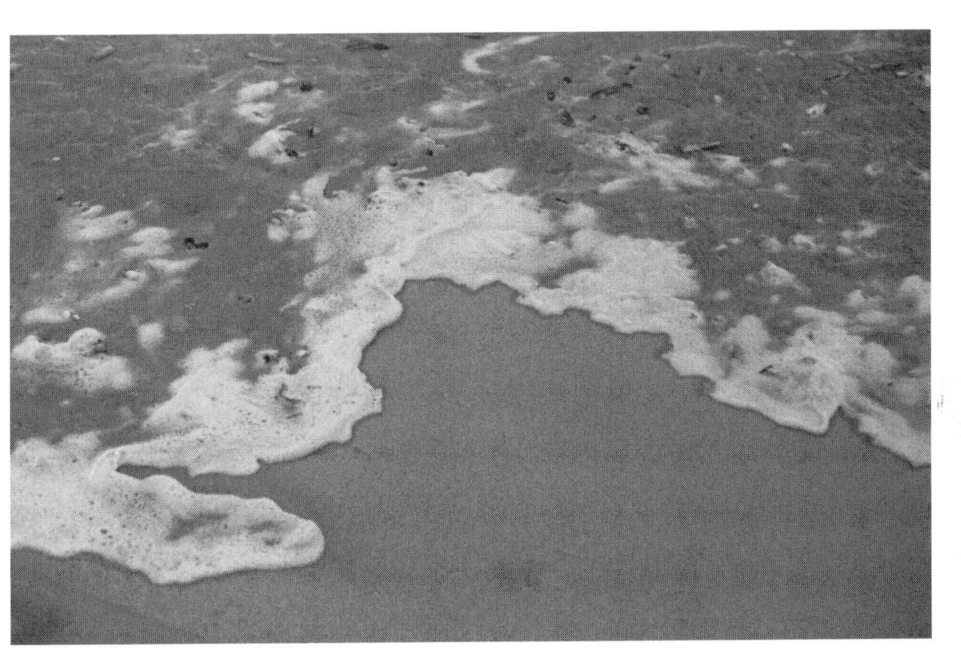

We're sitting over bowls of noodle soup in what feels like it could be a normal date anywhere between a man and a woman, but it's made to feel different because for whatever reason timespace has folded or collapsed or created a shortcut to pull us together.

I don't know why I booked that ticket to Tokyo a week earlier.

I had some time off work, I had the itch to go, there was just a voice whispering in my ear, and so a week later we met on the street near Omotesandō.

I sought reasons to stand closer to him. As he held open a map, I leaned in to study it, letting my arm graze against his as I pushed the crease flat and pointed at some metro stop. The small hairs on our arms intermingled, snapping like electricity across wires. I didn't move or make commentary, I just let the hairs tingle and he did the same, and there was that beauty of a moment when you realize that no one's pulling away. Maybe, I think, the only point of our time on earth is to live in search of that breakable awe.

We agreed to meet again after he finished his work at the church, and when we do, I'm charmed that he's got the awkwardly respectful behavior of a man on a date. His trepidation mirrors my own and puts me at ease, and the calm excitement we generate creates a closed kingdom of immediacy. There's that carefulness at stake, the balancing act of realizing that I'm not doing anything special; I'm just being myself and it's working. His eyes sparkle at me and I'm filled with life, I mean love, I mean life.

There is something mystical to me about him, maybe because I've never before met a minister my age. My mental construction of a minister has been someone old, pious, and remote from humanity, some holy figure preaching from a pulpit. But he's warm and approachable and endlessly patient with my infamous willfulness.

We start over a glass of wine, and I ask him how he got into ministry and he asks me about my writing. When I tell him about the novel I've been working on, he seems far too impressed and I wish he wasn't. Maybe it's because I don't think there's anything to be necessarily proud about for working on a novel, though possibly in finishing one, but maybe it's just embarrassing to me that he's so enamored of everything I say and I'm not even trying. Maybe I've gotten too accustomed to hurling myself at impassable walls.

I tell him about my life in Amsterdam, and he tells me about his life in Tokyo, and there must be some registration of the impossibility of it all, but for the moment I'm just so in love with the tenuous thing that's happening between two people over noodle soup.

"I was completely broken-hearted when he left," I tell him. "Shipwrecked. But I couldn't be doing the things I'm doing now if I was still with him. I couldn't be the person I wanted to be; I was too trapped in my role in the relationship. I was the reliable one. I wouldn't have been an artist; I couldn't toy with madness or howl at the moon. I wouldn't be in Tokyo now, eating in a noodle bar. I'm surprised by it. I want to tell him thank you. Thank you for leaving me."

"Are you going to?"

"No, there's no point. It's just a thought for me to have."

Later, he kisses me on the living room floor, and over the next couple days we evolve into well-acquainted lovers.

But then I'm leaving again. We stay up the whole night, as long as we can, and I have this image in my head of him in a white cotton undershirt, holding me close and asking, "Do you really like a *minister?*"

I answer, "I really like a *man.*"

He melts, visibly, but all he can say is, "Wow."

If I could bottle that emotion, it might be all I'd ever need. I'm happy for him, that he feels so loved. I'm happy for myself, too. When we leave the bed that last morning together, I go to the airport and he goes to church.

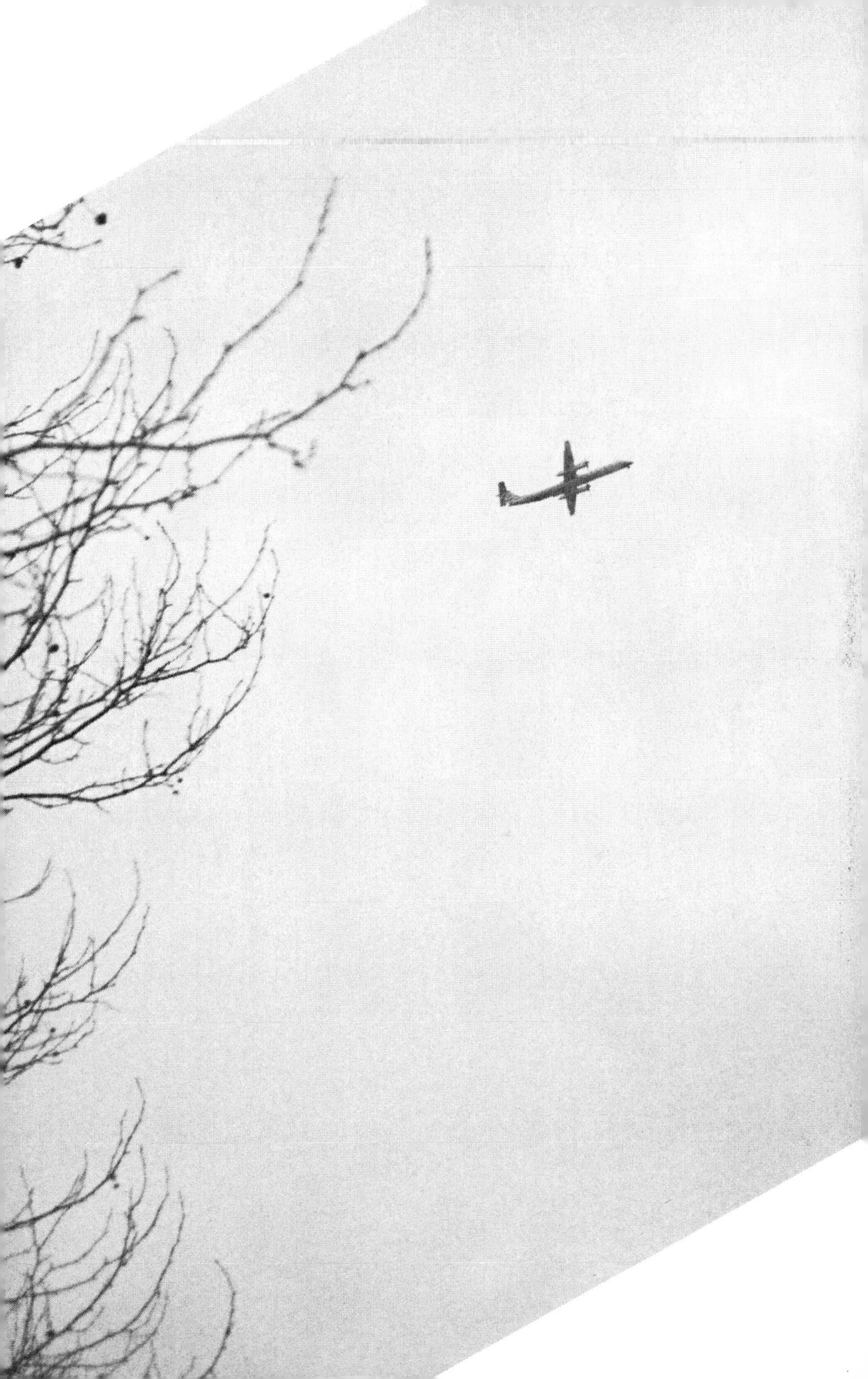

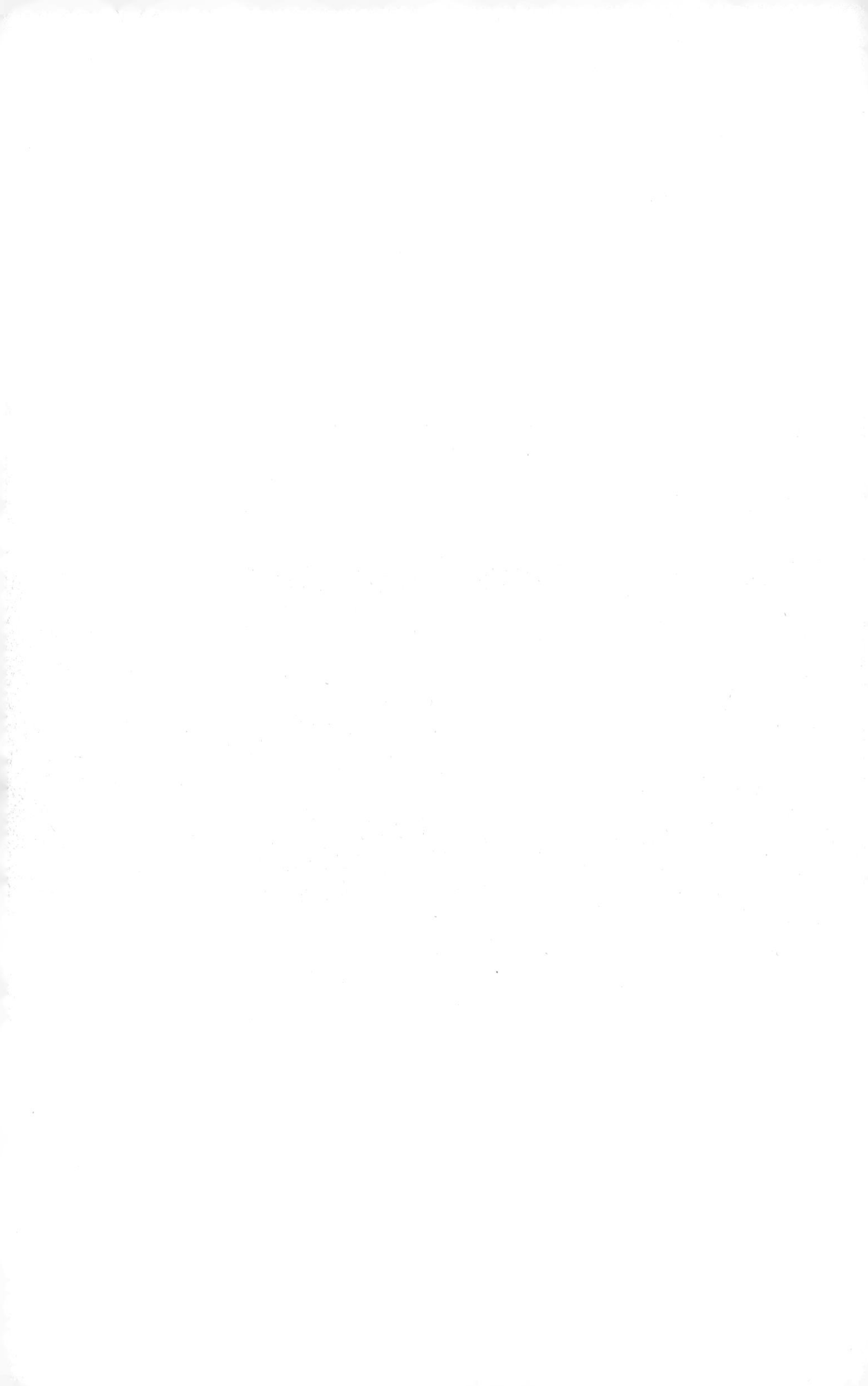

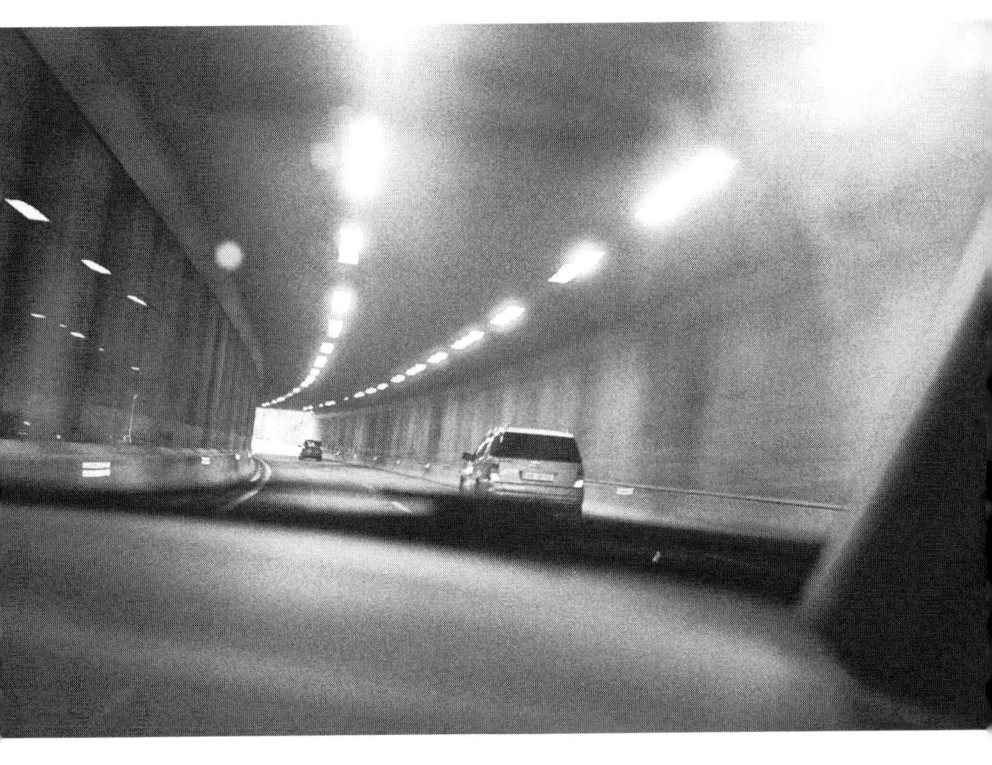

These things

in order.

don't happen

When it comes to what happened when, I don't have the same opinion as time, though maybe you're more inclined to believe time's side of the story, as though it's more objective.

If I loved him, I loved him always and forever, but just not at the moment. It was only because he was looking at the wrong moment that he didn't feel loved. It's not like the sun ever stops shining just because we have night.

I can go back anytime I like to that place, I mean that time. I can visit it with such ease and bask in the warmth of knowing love, of loving love, of being love with my whole body. But I've already been there. I've already been then.

It's so much more interesting to be elsewhere.

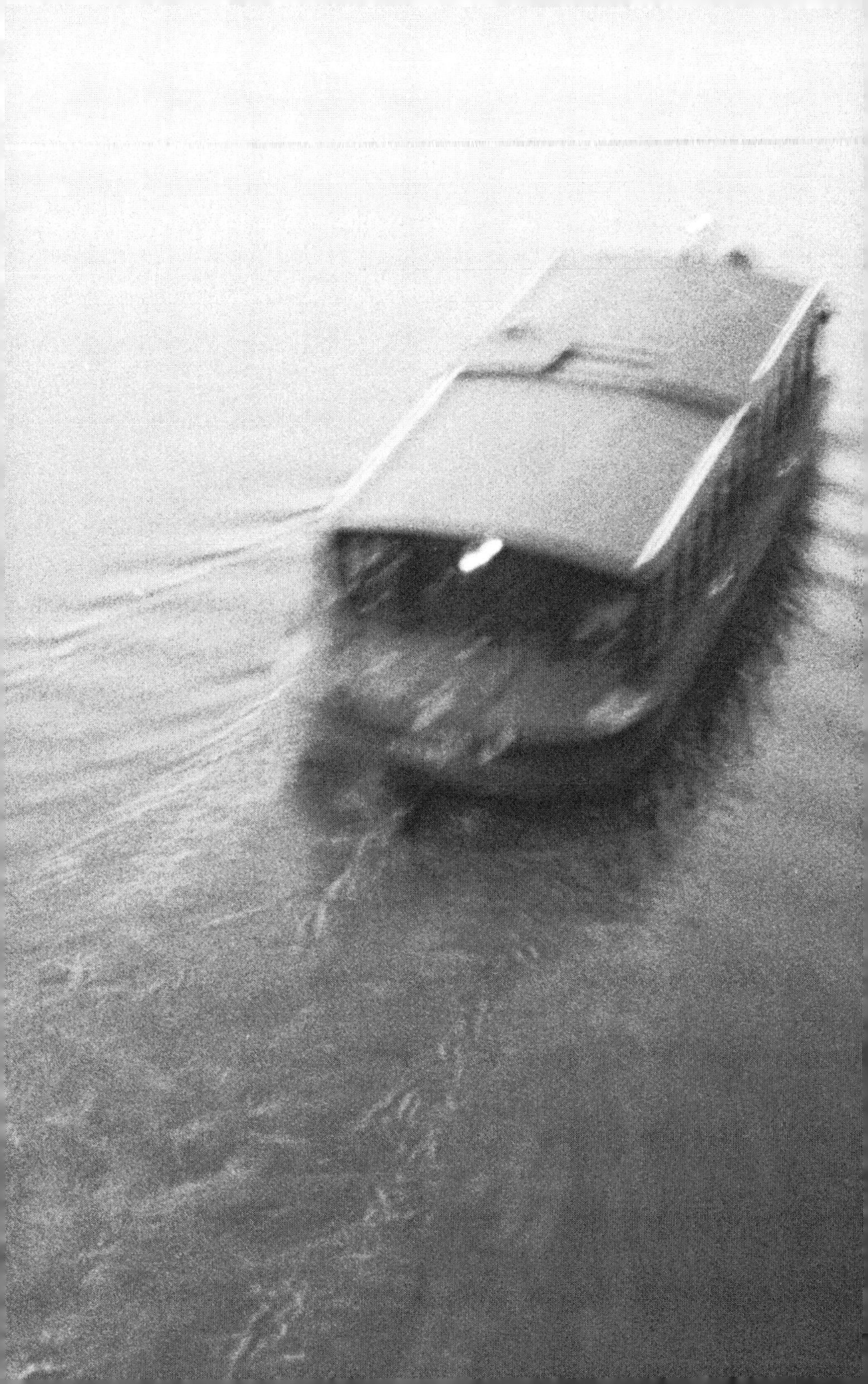

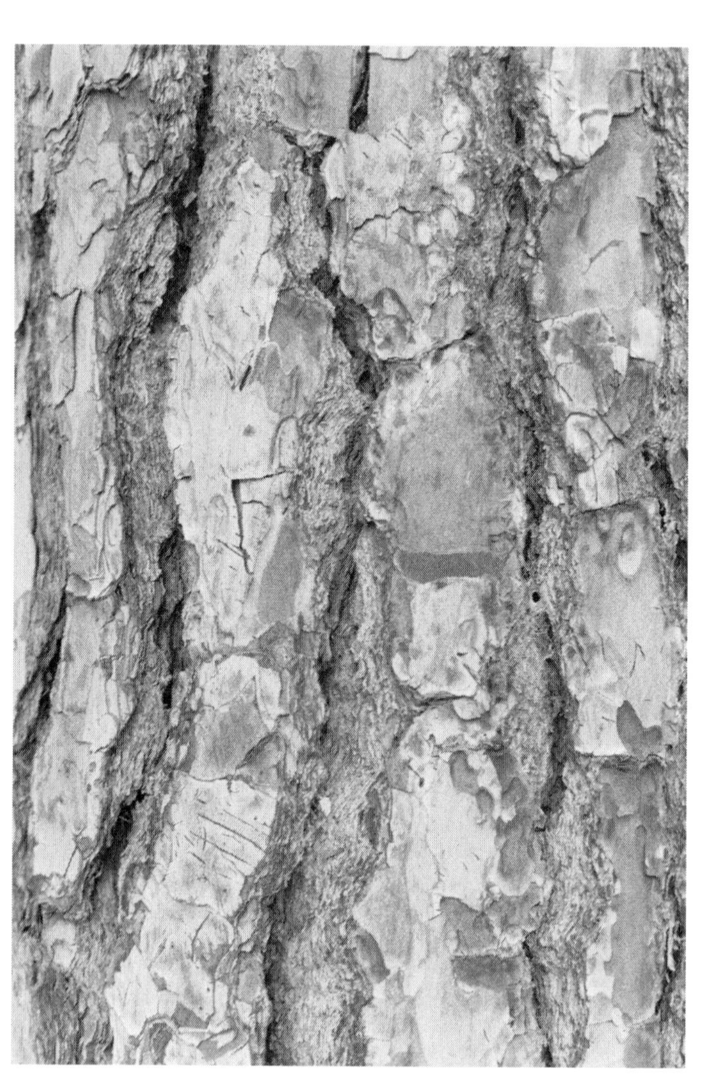

"YOU'RE NEVER COMING BACK," Molly said to me. We must've been eight years old, and I remember sitting under shadefall on the school playground when she said it but that can't be right.

For the last six months, my family had been living in Australia, and when we came back to Texas for a visit, my best friend and I met up to play. I was already talking about the fun things we'd do together when my family moved home again, but she just looked at me square and said those words: "You're never coming back."

Where'd she get that certainty?

It wasn't from me. I was sure I'd come back and we'd be friends again.

The heart isn't born knowing how to manage pain, it has to learn somehow. Maybe she was protecting herself from hurts unspoken. Maybe as I comforted myself with the knowledge that I would come back, she comforted herself contrary.

She was wrong, we did come back.

But she was right, we couldn't go back.

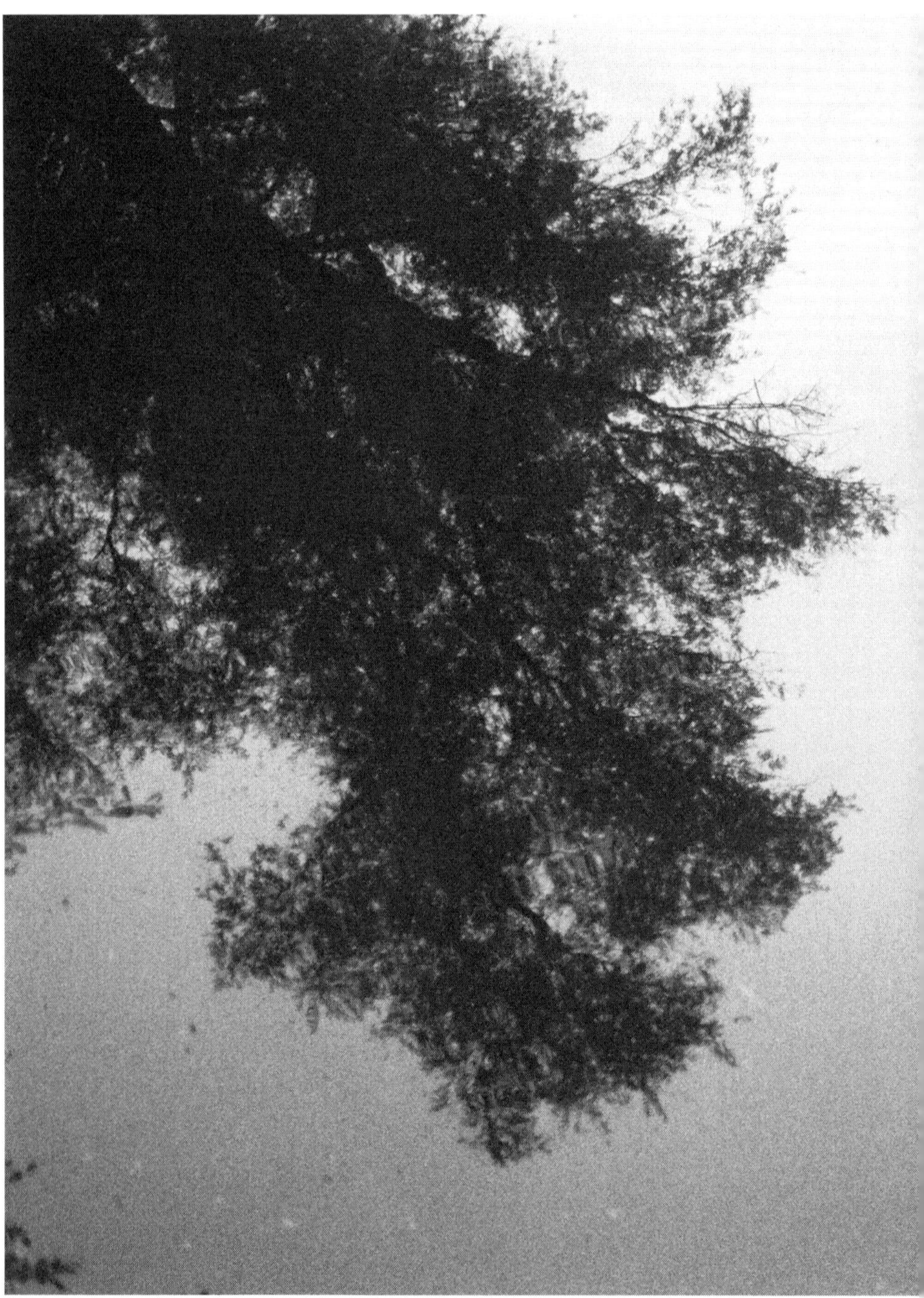

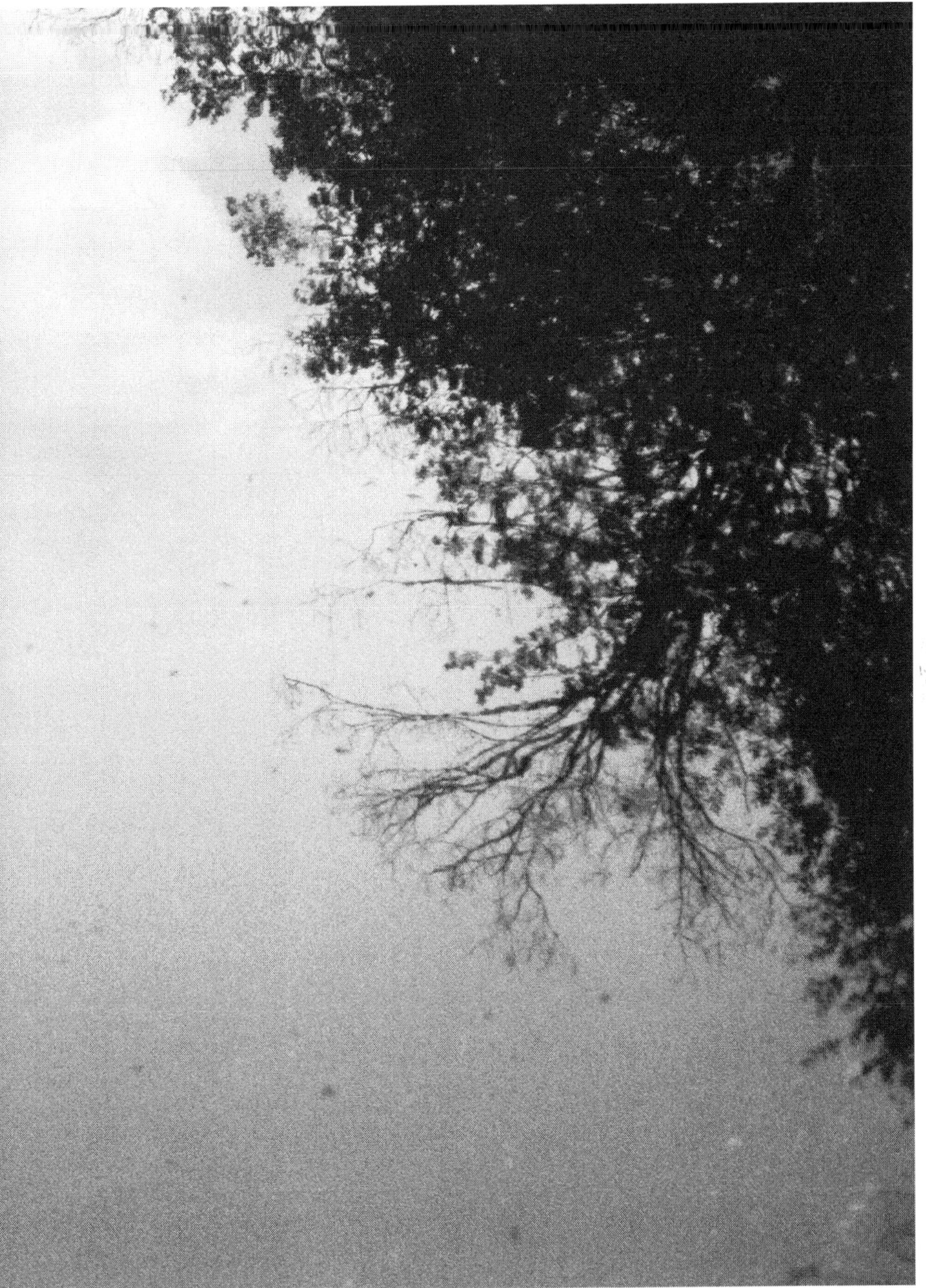

We're walking at the rate of an old man's shuffle, but I don't mind. Paul, as he introduces himself though it doesn't sound much like a Maltese name to me, starts to tell me about himself. Within the first block I learn that his wife died more than a decade ago and she was very good in bed. The way he mentions this suggests it might be why he married her, or at least it's what he likes to remember most about her. I smile as he tells me about her, and wonder what his life is like now without her.

I was standing outside a restaurant somewhere along the coast near Sliema, scouting the menu that was hanging near the door. It was too early for dinner, but I didn't have anywhere else to be. Paul came out of the neighboring door, where he lived above the restaurant and, seeing me standing there in my indecision, told me it was a good place. And just like that the conversation was started.

He asked if he could buy me a coffee, and I said sure. He said that he just needed to go to the pharmacy first and asked if I would mind accompanying him. Of course not.

So, we begin our shuffle together toward the

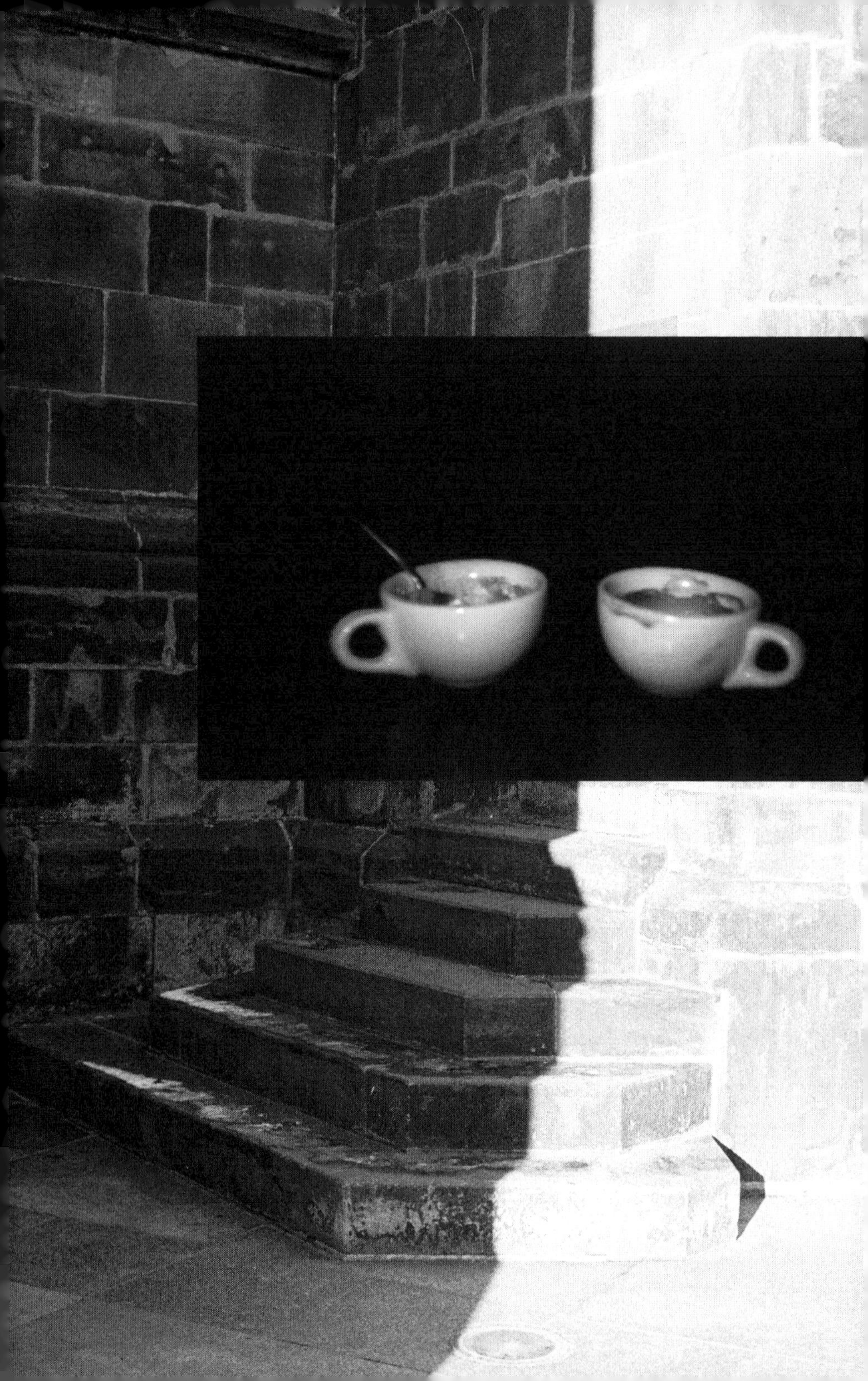

pharmacy, and I learn that he had slept with a great number of women before his wife, but she was very good in bed—this fact bore repeating.

As we sit and order a coffee it's clear the waiters recognize him, though they make no mention of it to him, nor to me. They just bring the coffees.

"Do you smoke?" he asks, pulling a wrinkled soft pack of cigarettes from his pocket.

"No, thank you," I say.

"You're a good girl," he responds, and places a cigarette between his lips. He fetches a lighter from his other pocket and brings it near, his hand shaking like a flag in the wind. He strikes the ignite several times, a pained look crossing his face. He strikes a few more times, the cool in his eyes delivering curses to his hand, but finally he gets the fire he needs. He takes a deep drag on the cigarette, the flame waving, to make sure the job is done. He sets the lighter on the table, landing it with a little extra slap.

He tells me that he was on the Olympic team when he was young, his voice dressed with pride even though he quickly appends that they didn't do very well, and I get an impression of how he might've bedded the women that he did. I get an impression, too, of why he started a conversation with me and feel a preview of sorrow for the frustration of ambitions that never quite fade.

"Your boyfriends must miss you while you're away," he says. I tell him I don't have any boyfriends, not that I want to encourage him but because I find it pointless to lie or misdirect. I tell him I've been single for a long time; I tell him I've had my heart broken and don't know what to do about it. I say it with a smile that shows that deep down I know none of it really matters.

He tells me about a restaurant nearby where I should have dinner and promises to escort me to it, though he insists he won't join me since he has other plans.

"Are you promiscuous?" he asks.

I smile at the word, something that seems so tied to a manner of thinking inconsistent with the intention behind his question. "No," I say and laugh, "I'm not promiscuous."

"That's okay," he says quickly. "You're okay, you're okay."

I drink the coffee and watch him smoke one cigarette after another and ask him about his wife who was good in bed but is now dead. They met in their thirties, and I suppose there was something about her that made her different from the rest. Now that she is gone... I could only imagine that other days are like today, he finds ladies to have coffee with and asks about their promiscuity, but who knows. Maybe I have caught him on a good day or a bad one. I wouldn't know the difference.

After we finish our coffee he delivers me to the restaurant as promised. He starts to leave, once again insisting he has other plans, but not before asking if I would like to see his apartment. This question becomes the line between suggestion and action that I am not willing to cross, and he understands. He says if I come back to Malta I am welcome to stay with him, and something about his tone impresses upon me that he doesn't offer it lightly. He takes the red paper napkin from the place setting, pulls out a pen, and starts to write out his name and phone number. His hand shakes with such severity that the pen can barely make the lines, so he steadies one hand with the other, and I try not to let my face betray the deep sympathy I feel for him at that moment. The letters are crooked and nearly unreadable. My own future passes before my eyes, when I will go through days aware that I've lost desirability and even relevance, when I will walk by people unseen like a living ghost. I want desperately for this to be a normal moment, when a man can simply write out his name and phone number for a woman and hand it to her.

"I will be very surprised if you call me," he says and leaves.

I place the napkin in my bag, flat against a hardback notebook, where no harm will come to it.

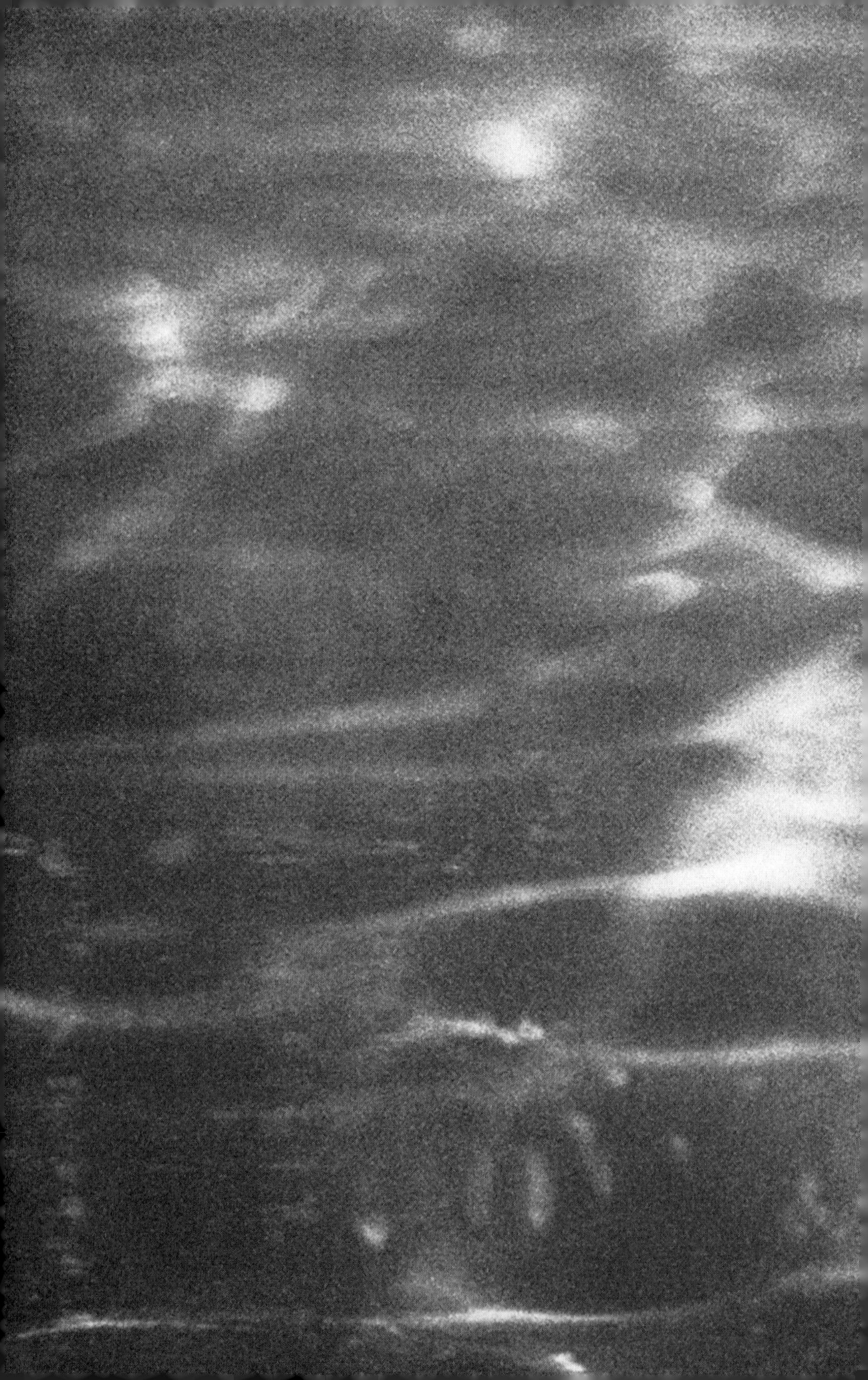

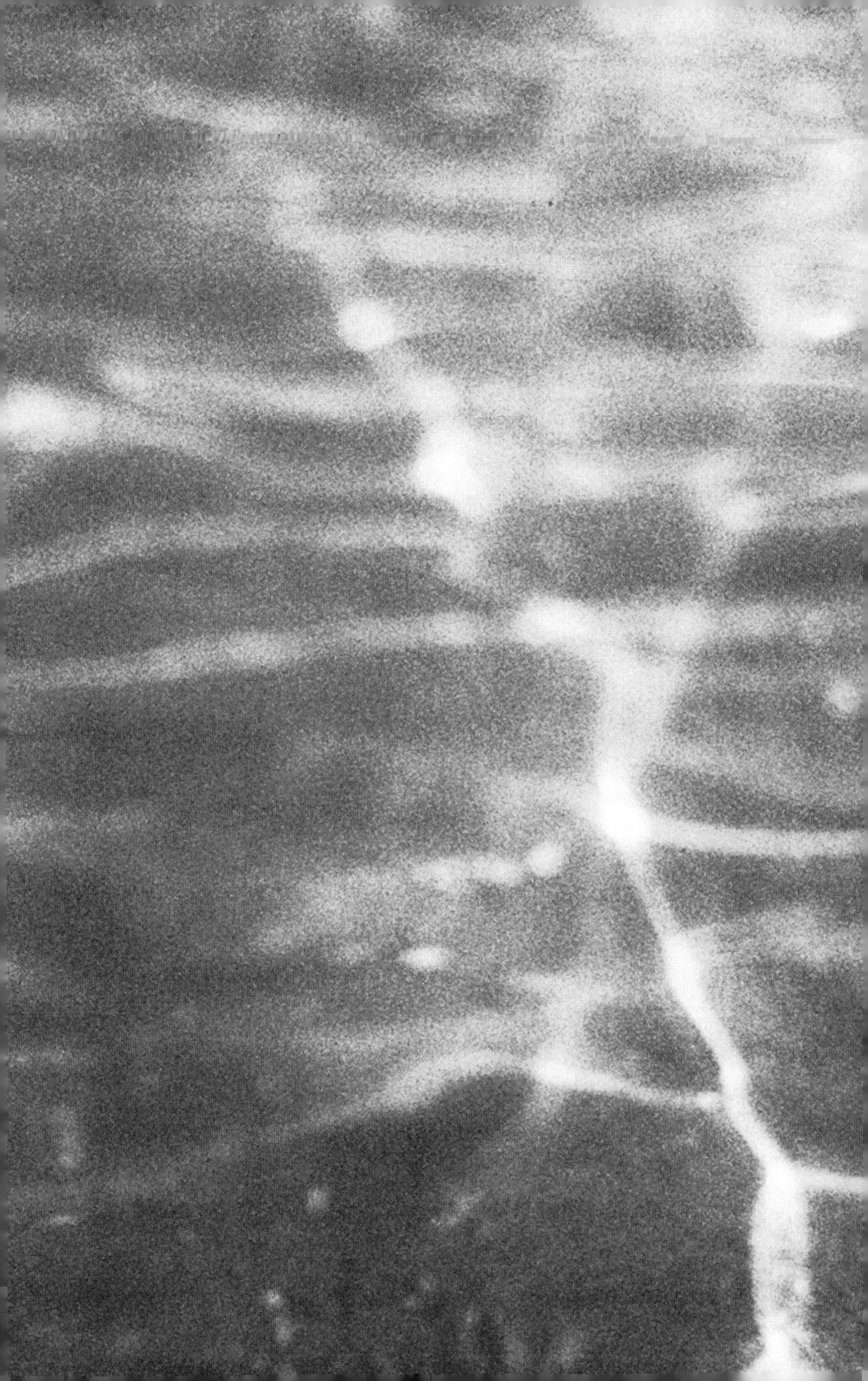

Spring had brought lush verdure growth along the path, small flowers and tall grasses that I ran my fingers through as I walked up toward the edge of a cliff. A local Maltese girl told me with flippant matter-of-fact, as I complimented the wondrous greenness of the island, that all of it would shortly be gone, sizzled into the ground as the sun worked its way into summer. It's crazy how you can fall in love with a place when it's in full bloom, never realizing, having not stayed to see the cycle, the way it burns its blossoms.

The walking alone was something better than nothing. Just the feeling of giving myself the mission of walking up the cliff to see the sights filled me momentarily with purpose. Day by day, at this point in my life, that was all I could hope for. I'd been laid out by a burnout and nervous breakdown at thirty that I then shook into a fantastic toxic cocktail with a breakup, with losing my job, with loving a married man, with trying to start my own company. For a couple of years I'd drink that cocktail down, vomit it back into the glass and then, because I felt so thirsty, take another sip, rancid fire down my throat. Repeat ad nauseam. It did its job.

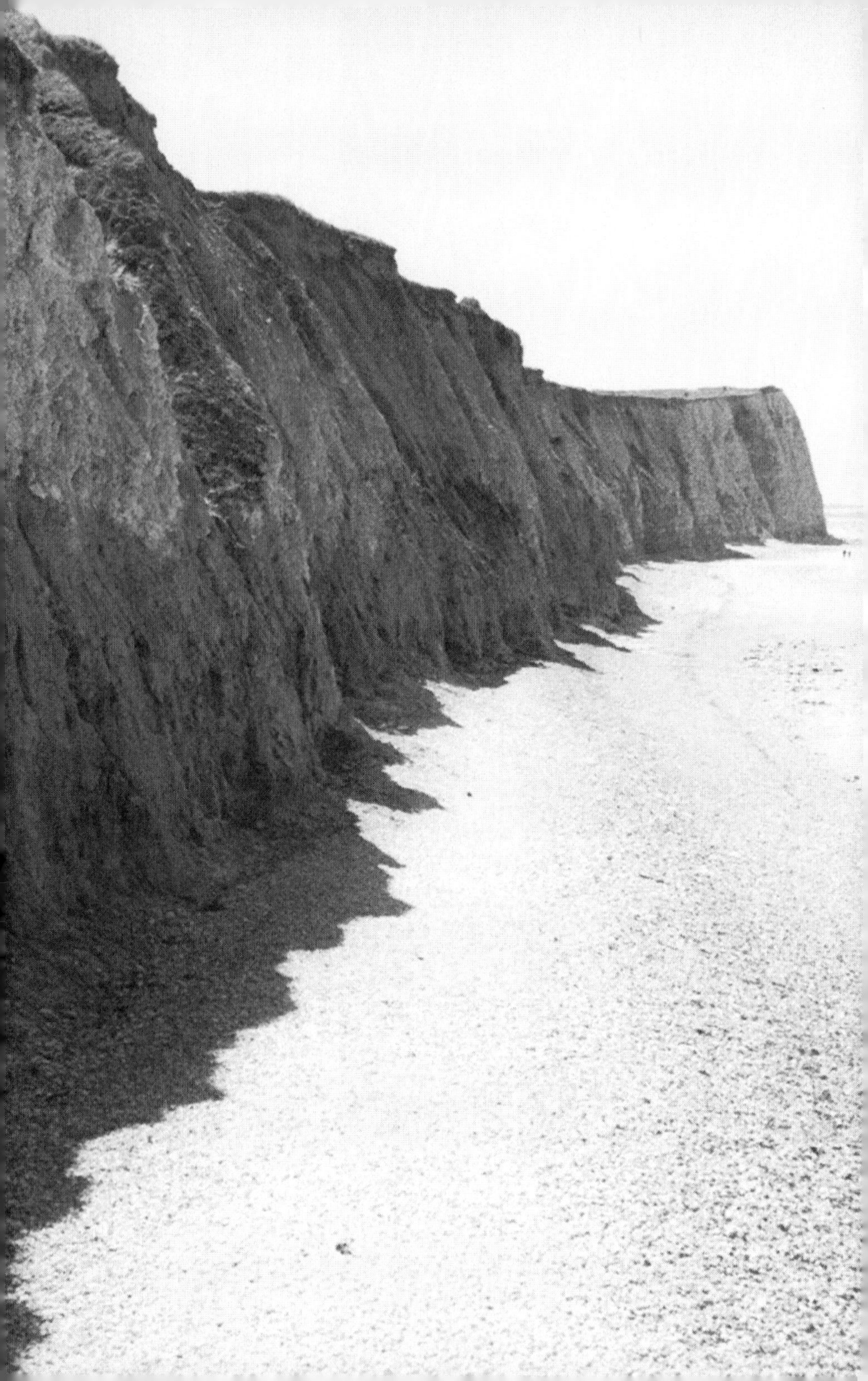

The beach below was nearly emptied as evening approached, not that it had been that busy on this particular day. I reached the edge of the cliff, and the crests on the current below were rendered small, cornered tips of light that vibrated in a musical pattern. "Feel something," a voice inside implored of me. "Feel something that reminds you it's worth being alive."

This searching was what had brought me to Malta, the faintest flicker of hope that a trip could trigger the engine into action again. I'd spent a couple of days with my friend Monica, but as she left the island the comfort she'd provided left a vacuum of time and emotion that I had to fill on my own. I went to the beach and lay in the sun, because that feels good sometimes. And lacking any brilliant new ideas of how to drag satisfaction from a rotting corpse of existence, I threw at myself the kinds of activities that had at one point brought pleasure. The same type of desperation that comes with eating according to routine long after the flavor has left the food.

I sat on a large rock at the edge of the cliff, which seemed to have been put there exactly for sitting and contemplating the ocean far below, and watched the sun descend slowly into the grey-blue water. I did not, despite my desire, feel anything aside from exhaustion.

There are not many moments in a lifetime that echo across time, that pronounce themselves clearly as decisive, both in the time they occur and then as you recall them later. I think of this moment now as one part of a twin.

On this Maltese cliff overlooking a beach, where I took in the great below from high above and tried to feel something but felt nothing, I told myself: Fine, be in this awful place in your head where you're at... but you're going to stay up here and watch the water until you want to live again. And so I sat, watching the tall grasses blow over the edge, watching the distant water sparkle, listening to the low and distant pulsing of waves crash against shores and rock, waiting until I felt sure that my brain would stop trying to attack my blood.

This moment's twin took place in Amsterdam as I lay in bed at night trying to fall asleep to escape the painful isolation and confusion I'd quagmired myself in. I cried, not in any desperate way but such that tears fell out of me like a faucet that couldn't ever be turned off, not really, and experienced the sudden and inescapable feeling that I didn't want to live anymore, that I was just done with it all. I felt something turn in my heart as something gave out that had been trying to hold on, like a safety switch suddenly yielding its tension, and I understood how easy it is to die of a broken heart. Since I survived to write this, you know I didn't die, not yet, but there it was.

I find it strange that I cannot remember with certainty which came first. These twin moments were within a month of each other; that's partly why I pair them. But when I try to come to terms with what happened when, I can't make it make sense. I just remember that... Well, I remember feeling that... I remember...

high enough to die
were you up high?
high enough to die

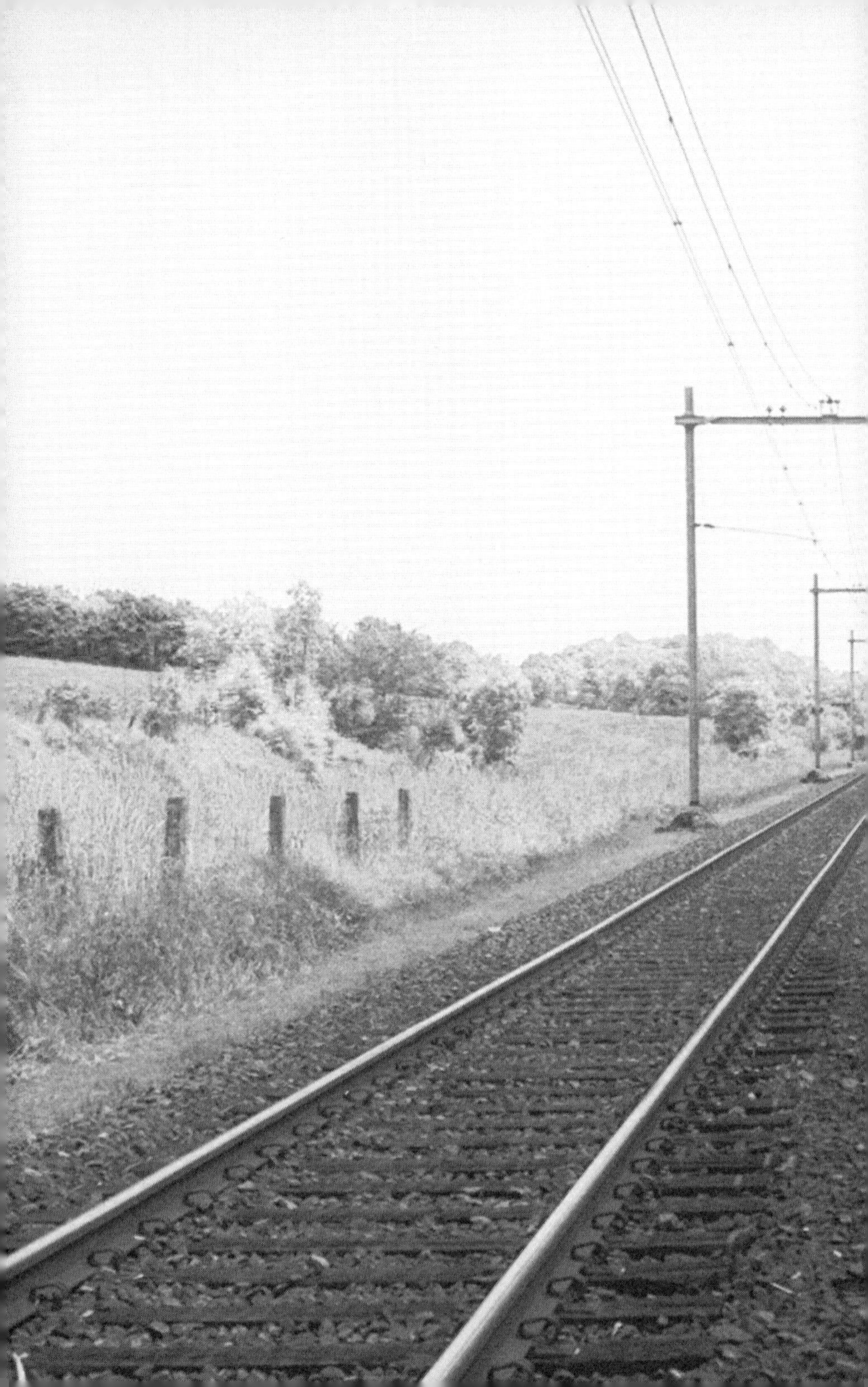

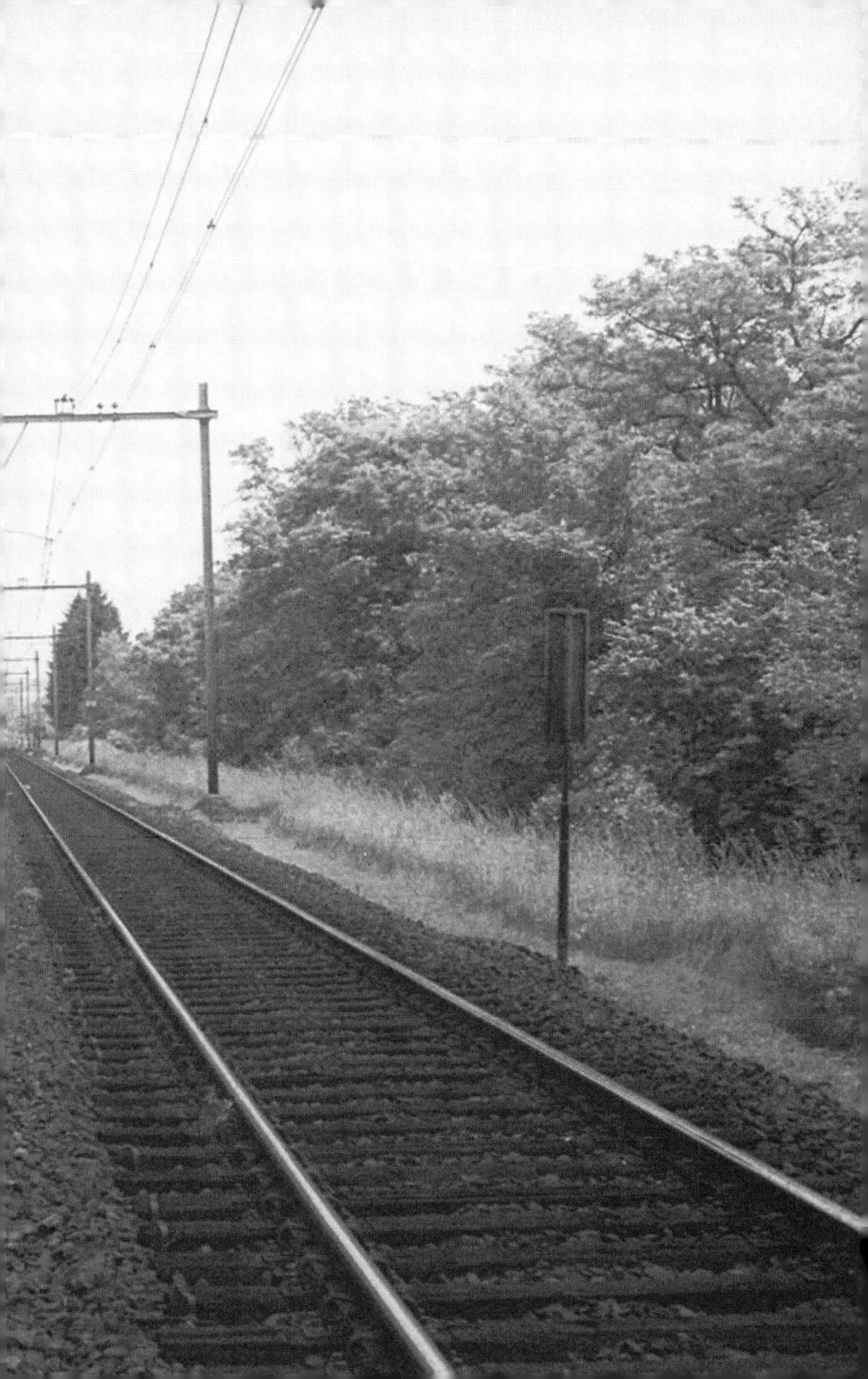

I'd pulled myself
out of the ash.

Clawing and crowing,
and like a newborn
I was crying, too.

Was this birth harder than the last? It's not a contest, it's just fighting for life, time and time again, until you give up or lose. And it's exhausting to be burned down to nothing, even more so when I know it was me who started the fire. Exhausting to rebuild, even more so knowing it will all burn.

Again and again, burn it down.

Again and again, build it back. Scars and healing and new skin.

With raw flesh, I make deals with spirits unseen for that to be the last time, I just can't survive that again. Then, with feathers bright and alert, I start pecking at flames that made their move but couldn't quite finish me. I say, "Hey, you remember me? That was wild, we should hang sometime."

Camus said we must imagine Sisyphus as a happy man, but all I can think is that he got off easy with pushing that rock. There will be more fires in the future, and it's hard knowing how it's going to hurt. I must imagine the phoenix to be a happy creature.

I'd pulled myself out of the ash, and I was proud and even though I was humbled I was cocky. Every time was triumph.

When my feathers grow in, shouldn't I fly? Shouldn't I?

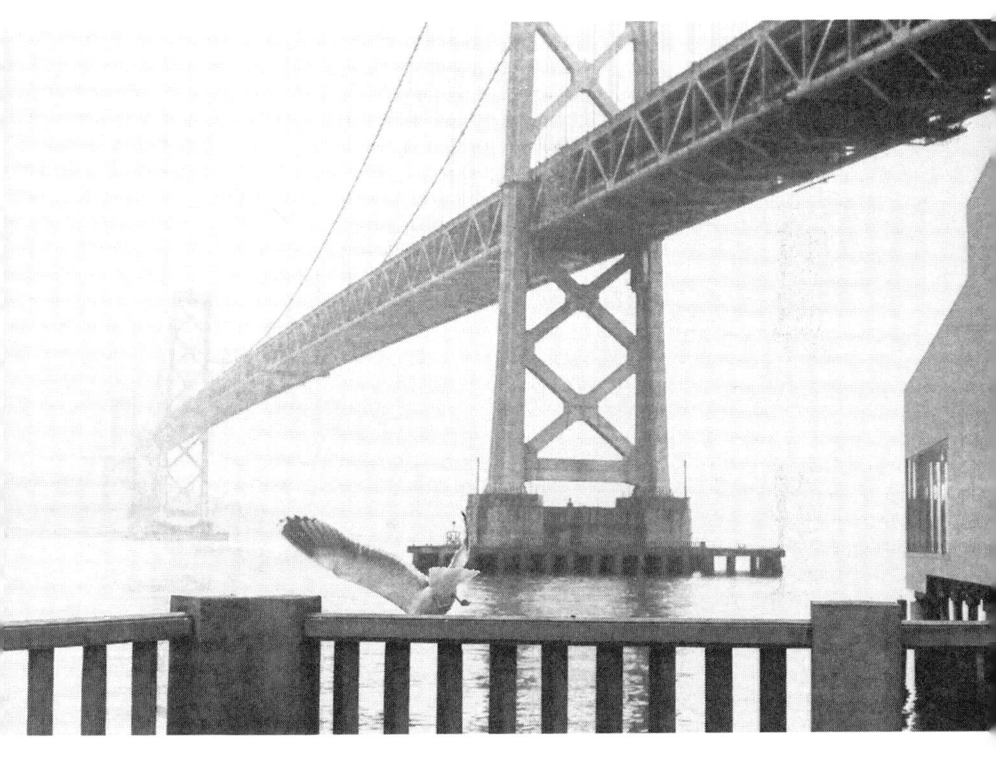

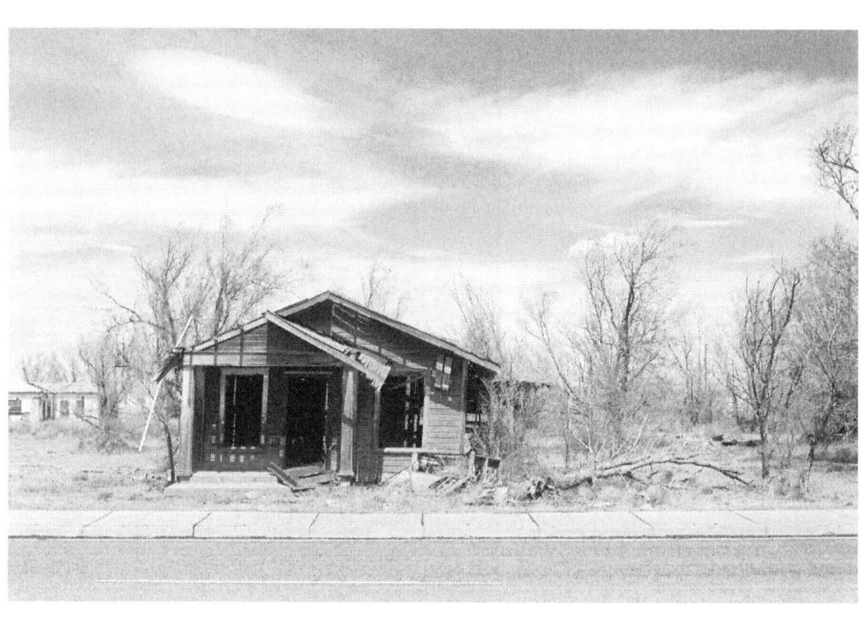

"Oh, I sent you a box," Mom says on the phone.

"Yeah, I got it. Some posters I had in storage." The box had lain on the floor for a week, I didn't even want to look at it. "I'm not sure why you mailed it to me though."

"I was cleaning out the garage and I found them."

A week earlier, I'd come home from work to find a long poster box waiting for me in the stairwell. I grew warm with promise at the unexpected surprise. They must have found something, maybe at one of the museum gift shops they're always going to, and mailed it over.

Opening the box, I instead found several posters that I recognized. Things I had bought years ago, which must have been sitting in storage in Austin at my aunt's house and collected by my parents when they got their own things out of storage. Included were two posters I'd bought in Czech Republic and brought back to the U.S., somehow already fantasizing about hanging them up in my house someday, to reminisce my years abroad. Now, here they were, pushed back in my hands, another anchor pulled out of the water and it's all I can do to stay myself from keeling.

Their edges were tattered from being tacked into the wall and moved around and whatever other ill treatment the lifestyle of a young twenty-something delivers to posters.

"I don't see what good they'll do me here though," I say, not knowing what to say.

"I don't understand. Where would they do you good?"

"They were fine just sitting at your sister's, right?"

"Well, you're not moving back, right?" She speaks the words of a question, but her tone isn't asking anything.

A lifetime of her distance swells up in me. I could move back to prove her wrong. I should stay away till the end of time. Push, pull. Anguish at the ready.

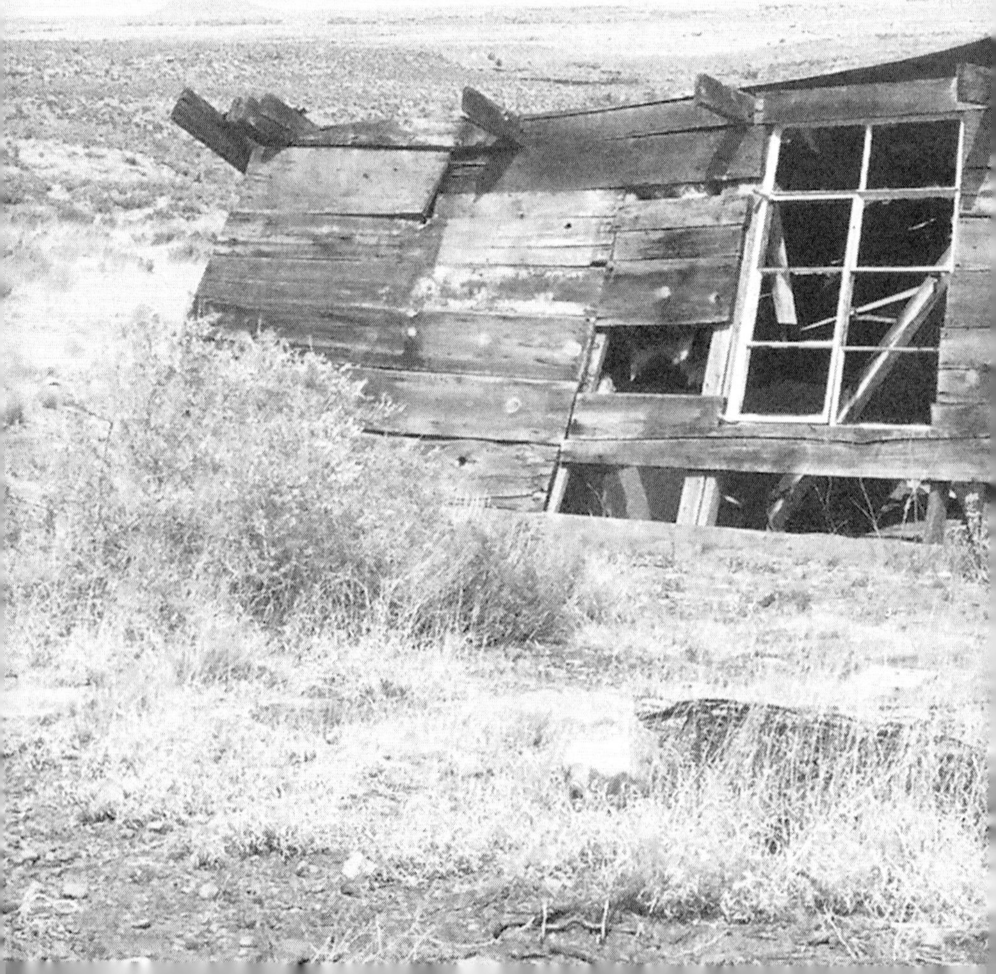

"Life is very long, Mom."

"Well, they were just sitting here in storage, and I don't want to move all this stuff again. I'm not sure what we're supposed to..."

"Got it," I say, eyeing the posters on the floor for evidence of the divide between value and junk. I don't want to possess it; I don't want to throw it away.

She values order so much more than sentiment.

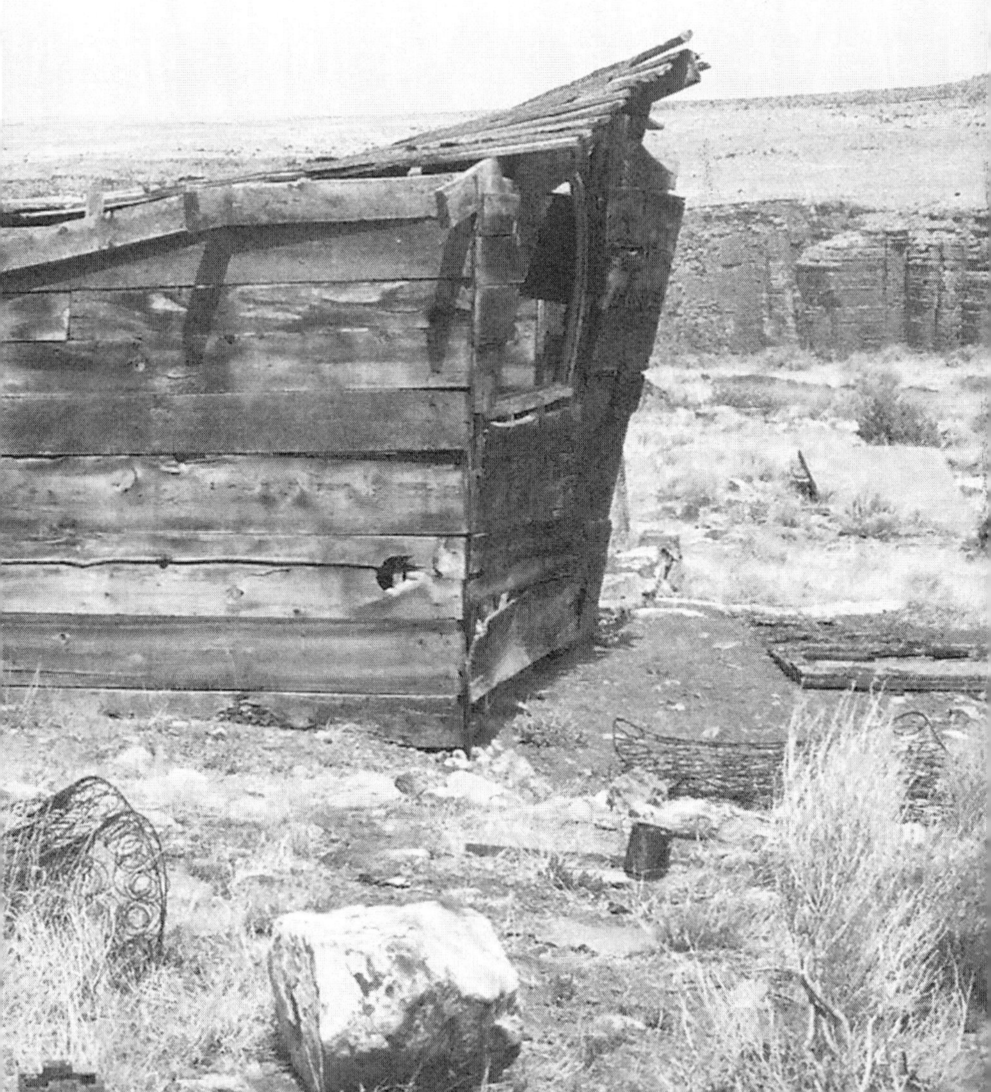

Let's set things straight: I'm not telling you

FACTS.

I'm telling you the truth and that's something different.

I leave things out. It's not like you need to know what I ate for breakfast this morning to know if I'm angry.

If you ask someone else, they might say I got it all wrong. And I don't mind that either, because I believe every word of this, I just mean it's true what they say, that we don't see the world as it is—we see the world as we are.

Everyone tells me I look just like her. I think for both of us, my mom and me, it's a mirror we don't want.

Unified

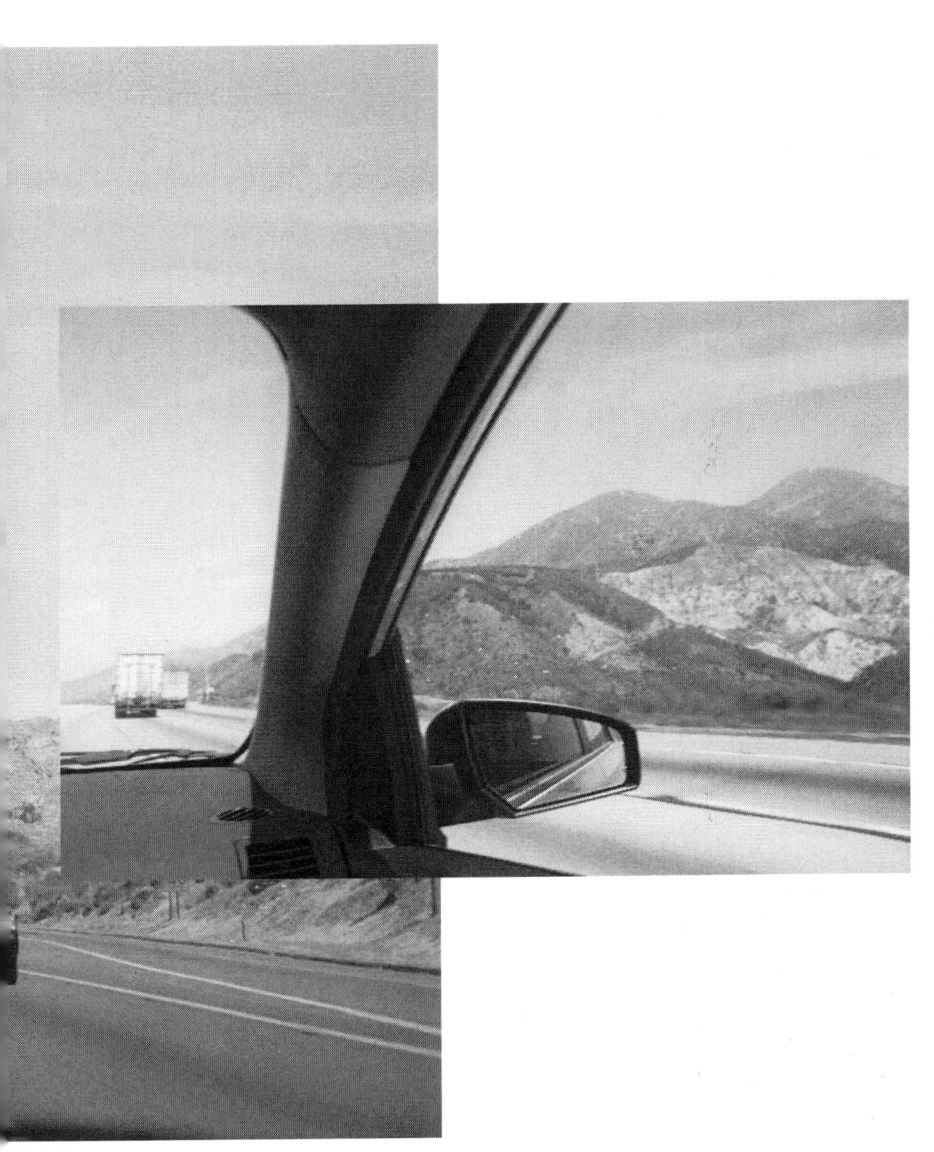

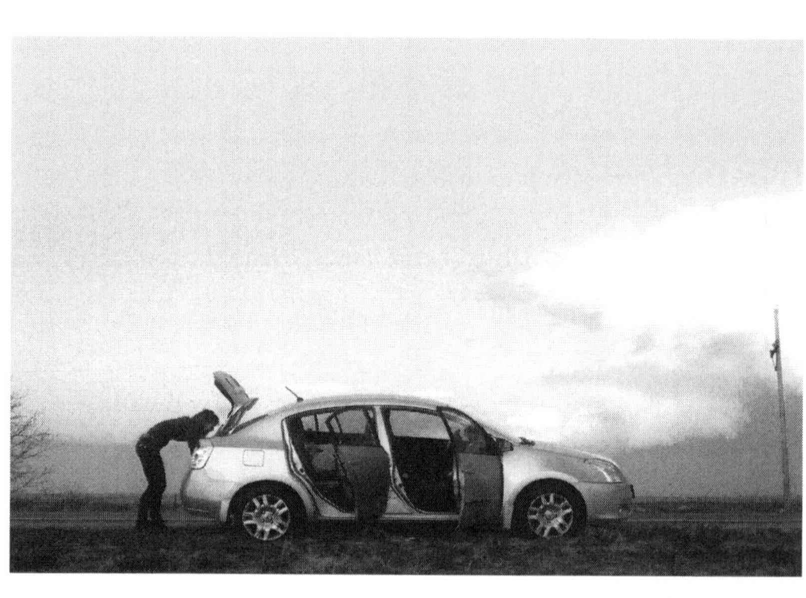

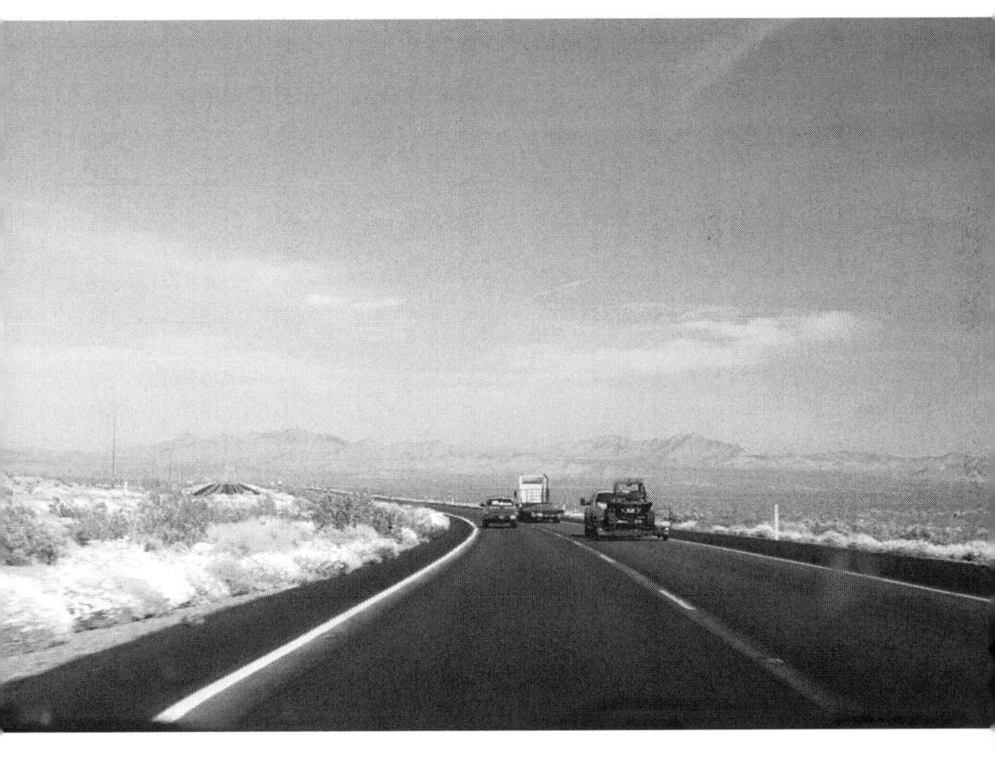

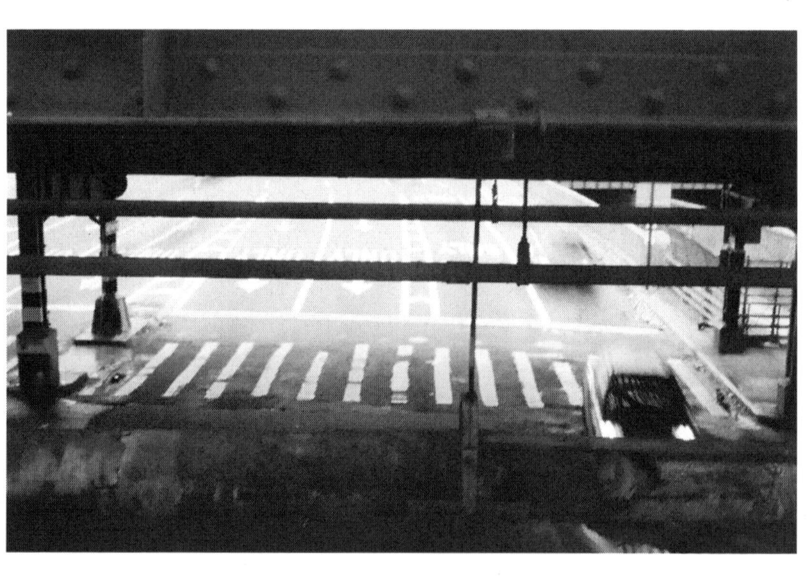

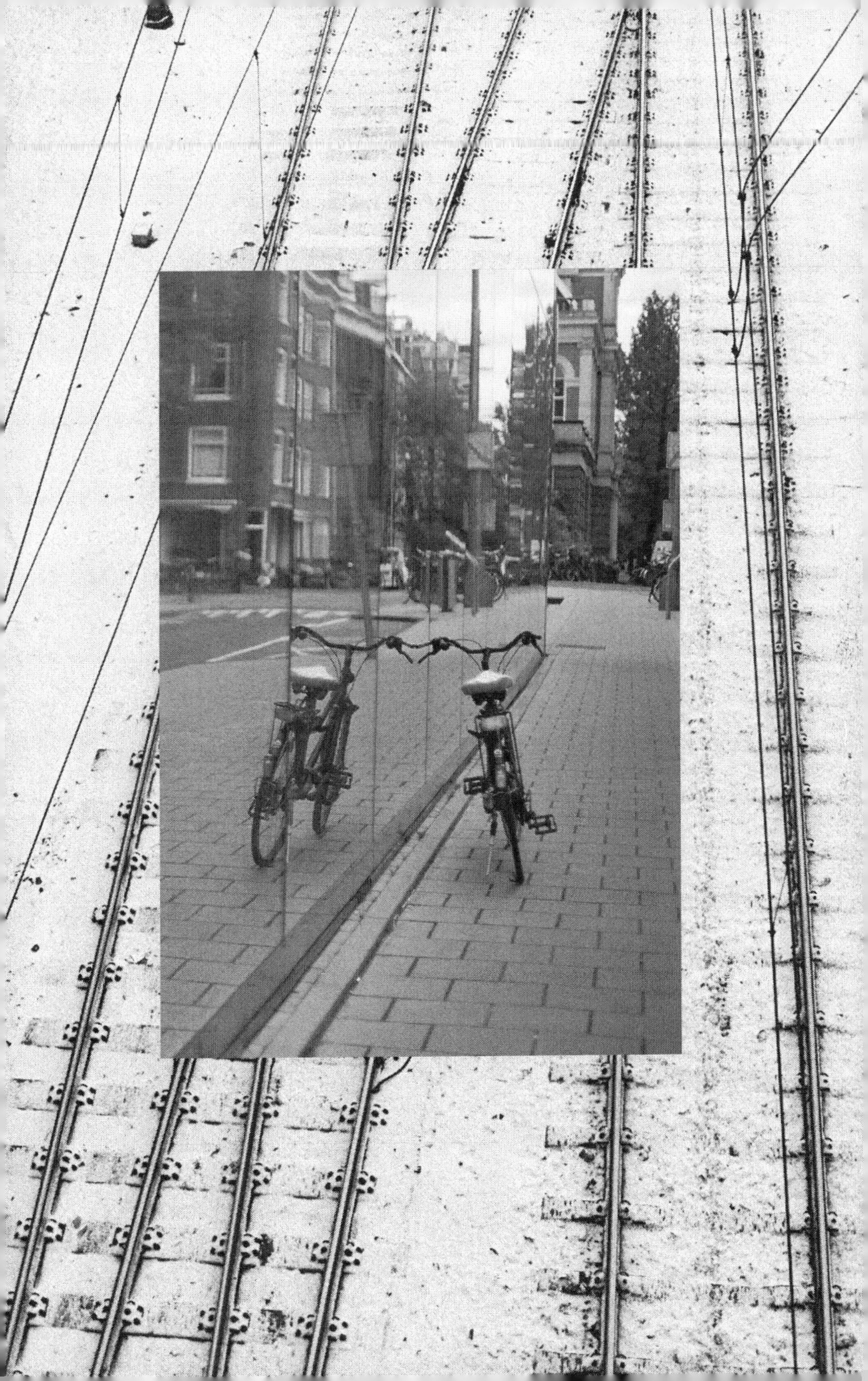

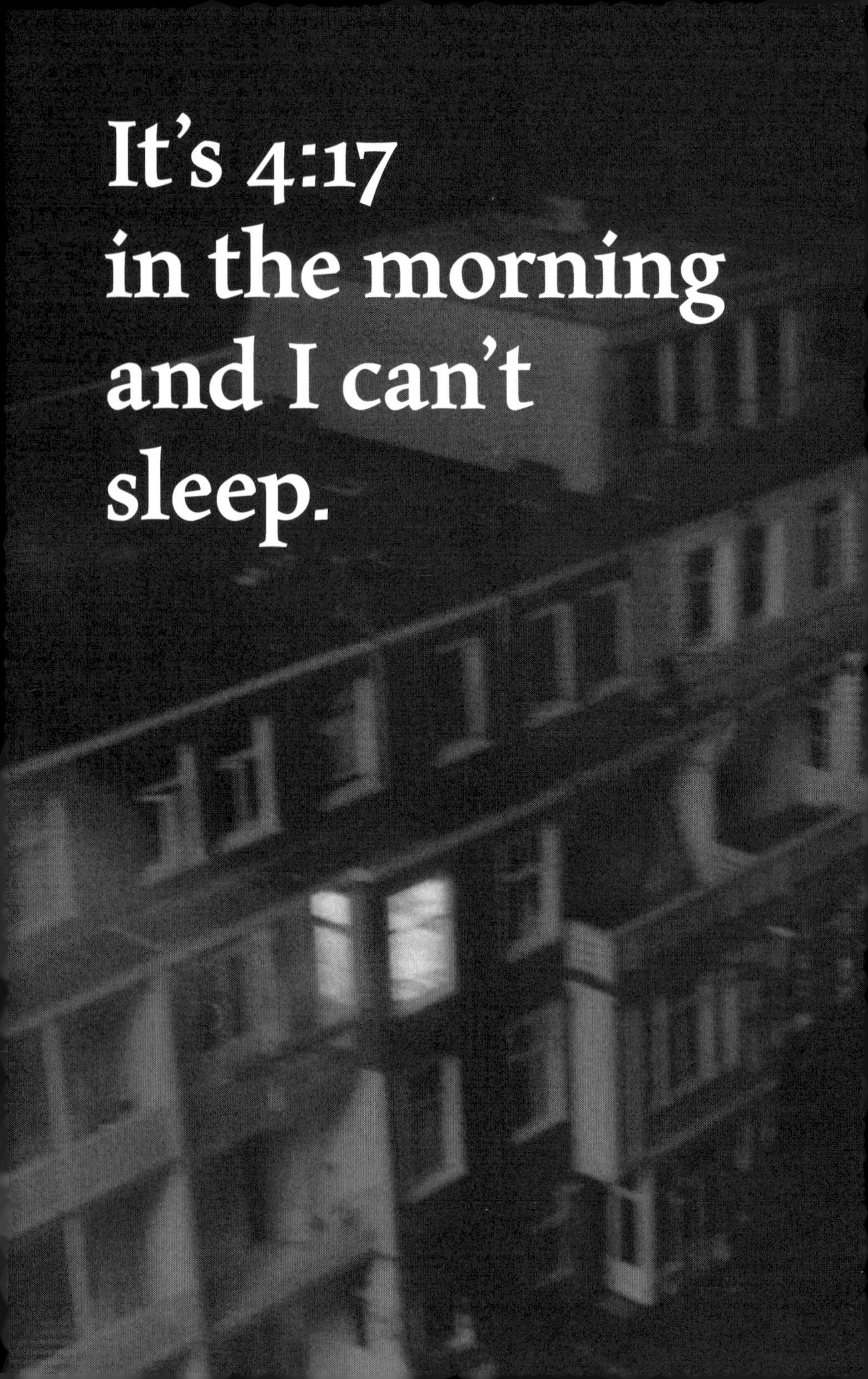

It's 4:17
in the morning
and I can't
sleep.

I can see from the glow in the next room that Lake is also awake – I don't know why the hell I thought that chai helped you fall asleep – but I don't call out to her; I just feel comforted by her presence.

Anytime I got to thinking that I spend too much time on the move, I only had to look at Lake and realize I was still okay. I loved having her stay at my place as she passed through Amsterdam. She was a traveling home, and with her there I could feel in and out at the same time.

Usually, I'm out like a light. So, the times that I do have problems sleeping, I just spend soaking in demons. All those dark corners of my head come out to play.

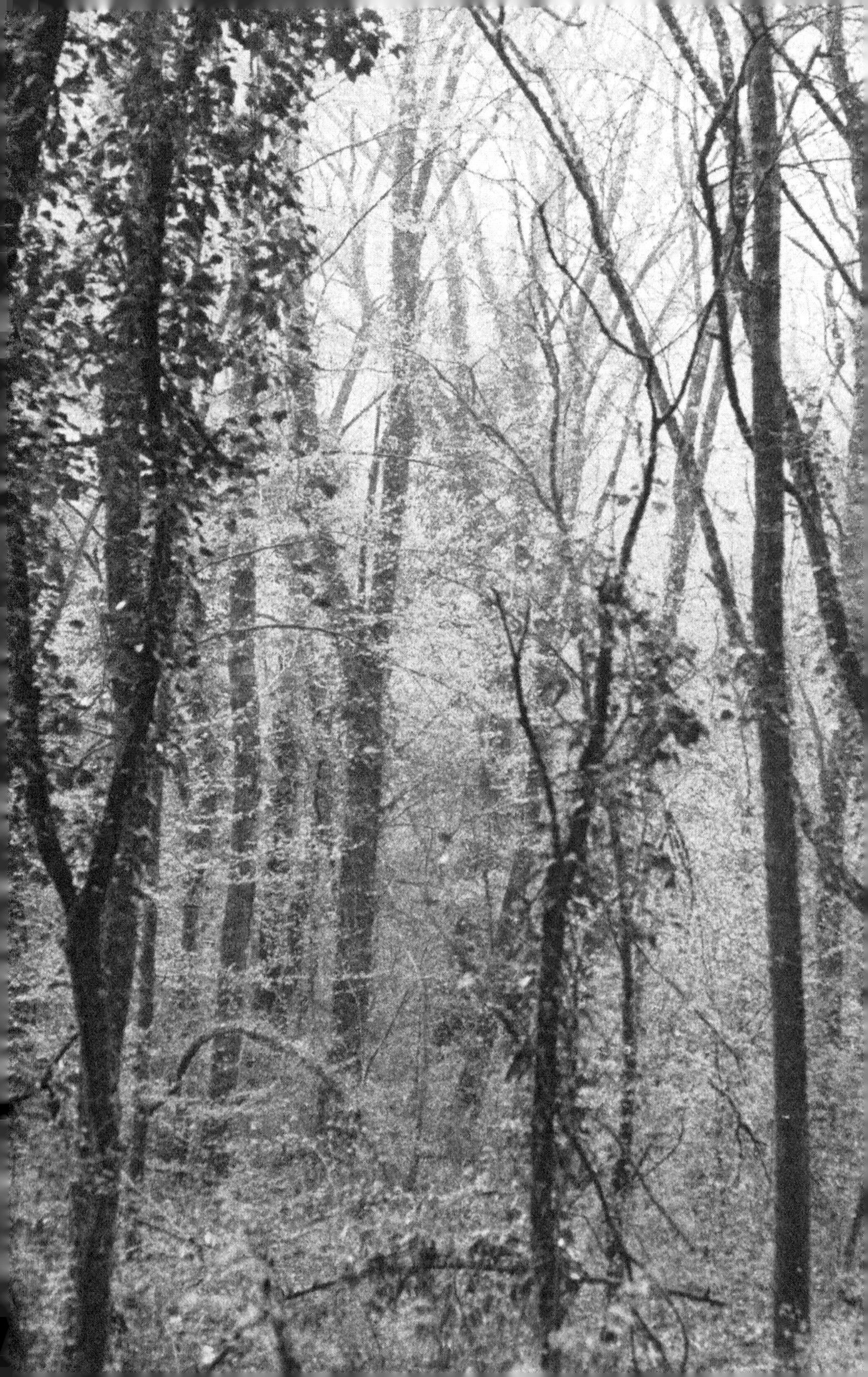

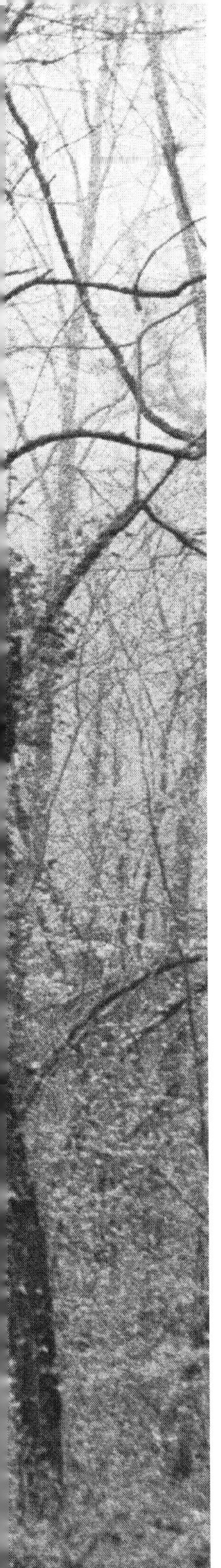

Lake is like me, a Texan with pieces of her heart scattered around the planet. She always seems to me so full of love and woe, the likes of which make me ashamed for feeling sorry for myself. Maybe she says the same about me. She's adventurous but she moves around with devotional languor, taking her time and giving it to others.

She tells me: "I walk around with a monkey on my back called loneliness, and sometimes I feed her some peanuts and say 'Hey sugar, you doin' alright? You need anything?' and she says she needs some loving, but that's what she always says, that's her job."

In the morning, I wake up and Lake's already awake with her headphones on, clicking around on the internet that takes her anywhere. I'm not so sure she's slept at all, but she doesn't look tired.

I heat up the coffee pot, and I see her turn her face away, toward the window, as she sniffs. I know she's been up crying and doesn't want me to know, doesn't want to be a bother. I move leisurely around the apartment, going about my business with the coffee pot and pouring it out, and then when I have two cups ready, I come and sit next to her on the couch and say, "What's this abyss you're falling into?"

She takes the cup of coffee and says, "What abyss?"

And I don't mind her playing dumb; I just let it be and say again, "The abyss you're falling into."

"You can see it, huh?"

"Yeah, I recognize it."

She's had a hard time of things, but it's not my business to get into that. Those are her heartaches to conquer and write about, to sing about on the stages of darkened cafés. But she's paid for it to move around; she pays for it every year that goes by, more than I. There's a wide, aching chasm between movement as an idea and the real emotional cost to leave something behind, irretrievably.

I ask her, "Don't you miss living here?"

And she looks thoughtful and forlorn and says, "I do miss it. But I don't mind missing it. It gives me something to return to."

I know what she means, and at the same time I wish she didn't feel it. I want her to come back, and unlike so many of the people in my life, I tell her so. "I wish you'd move back here. I miss you."

"I miss you, too," she says. "But I feel safer knowing you're there. It makes it okay for me to go out and see other things, too."

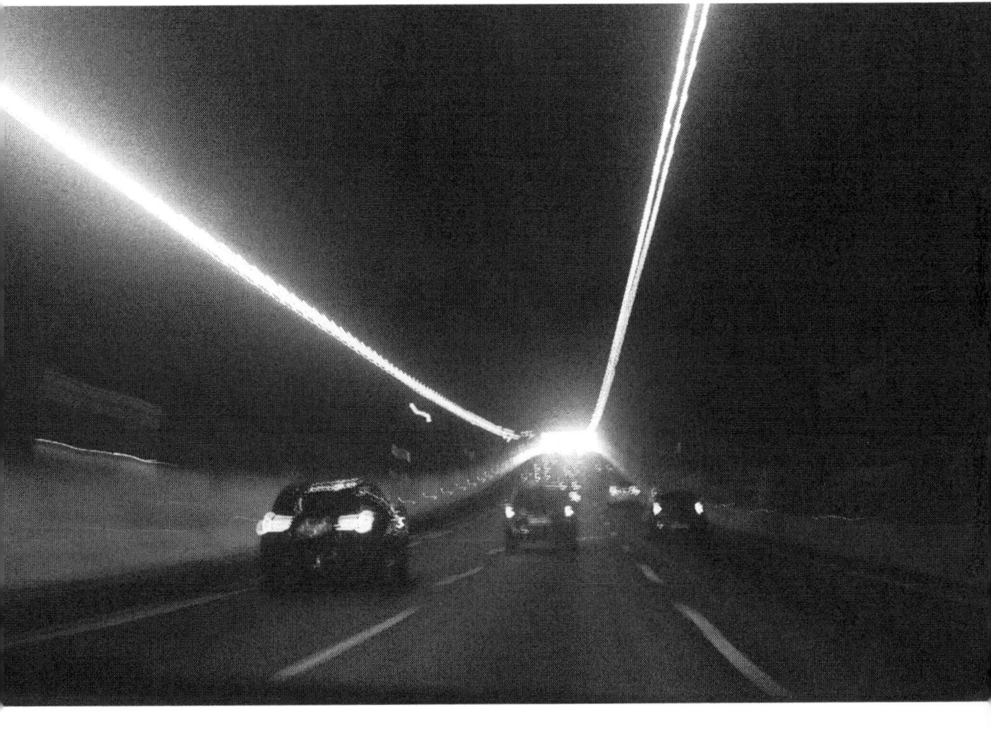

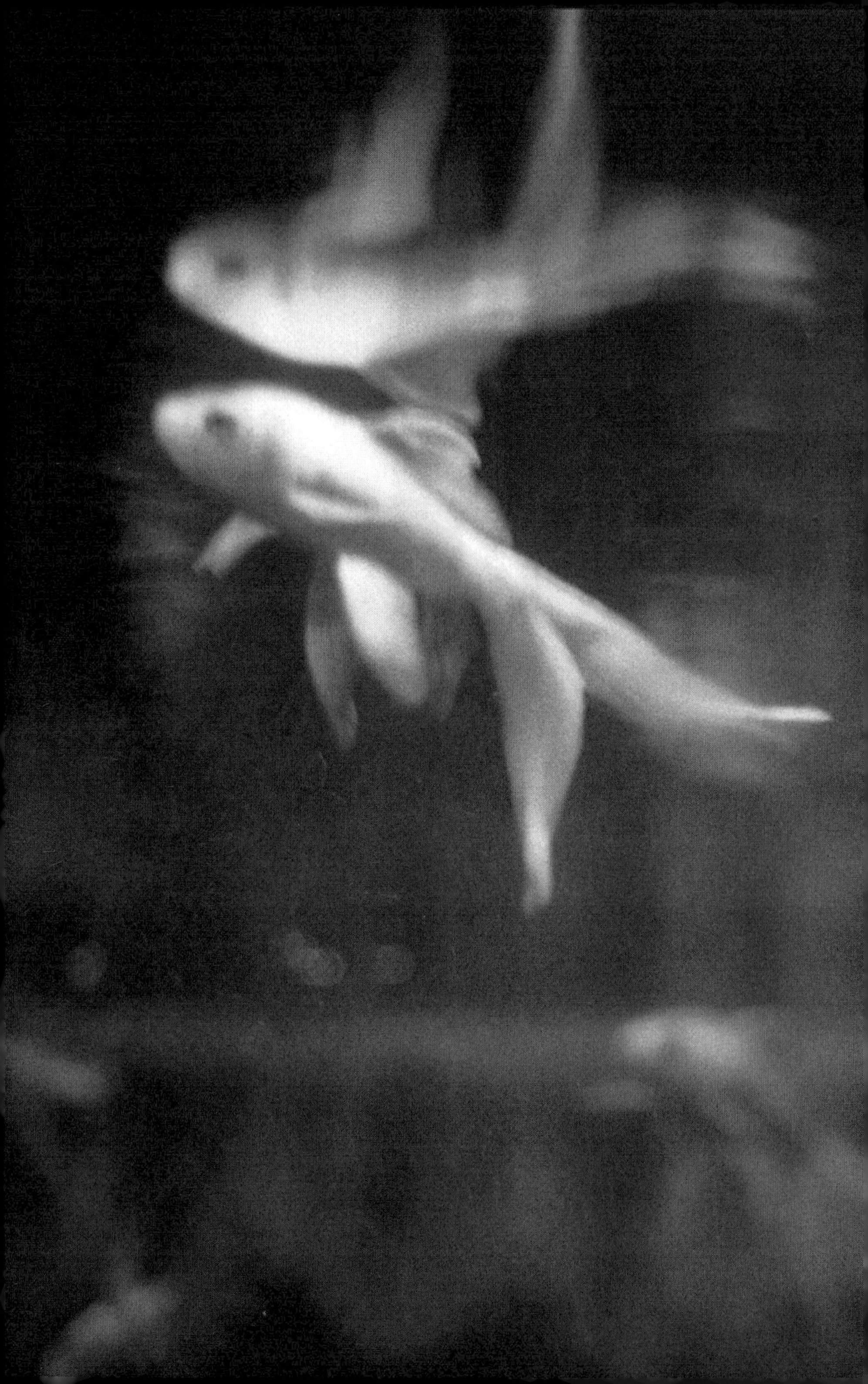

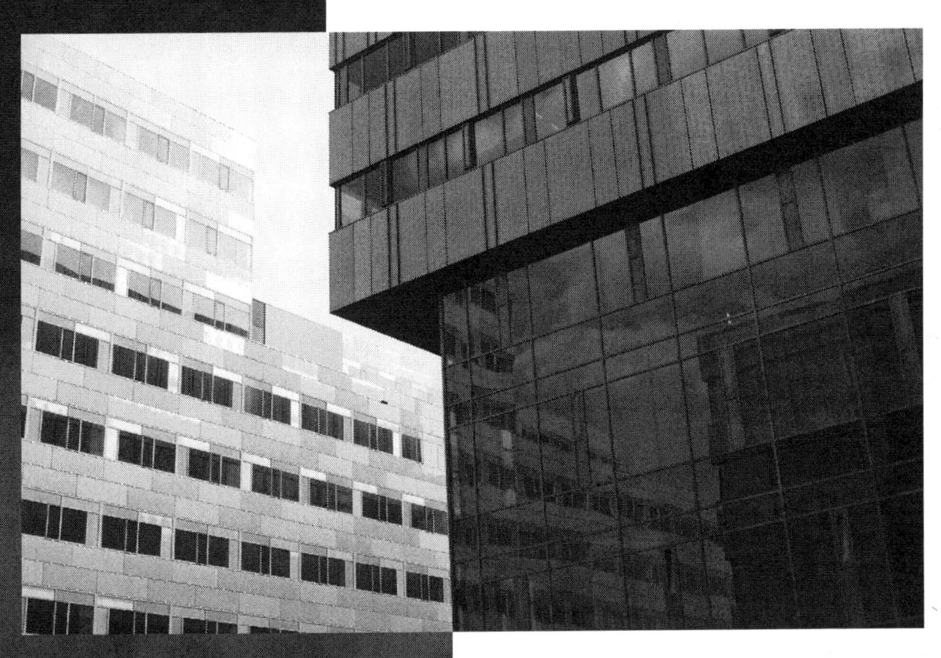

September in Amsterdam, and it's a hot summer day, strangely. Lake comes to meet me for lunch before leaving town. She's wearing a salmon-colored dress and walks in carrying nothing, her hips swinging and her arms loose by her sides, no weight at all.

We sit and talk about the love of work, the work of love.

Lake is at the tail end of something called love, coming out of its disaster, but she's got peace with it now, fueled by the contentedness coming out of the sunshine. She says she wishes she'd been single all this time, that it would have felt better. She might have gotten more out of it, she says.

That's probably true, I say, thinking of the time I spend alone as the densest, layered with complexity unachievable otherwise. For sure the most productive. My work has never been better.

We finish lunch and leave, Lake going one direction and I going the other. We say goodbye, and as we embrace I touch her soft linen fabric and inhale her smell.

I want to be the sort of person who doesn't mind that she's leaving again. I want to be the sort of person who knows how to let her be the best version of herself, free.

"Hey," she says to me, half-turned. "I believe in you. I'm proud of you."

And she turns away before I can say anything, going, but her smile trails after her like motion blur — I can see it, full of loving. It's genuine, and also gone.

I'm torn between places, burning red like time

Notes and Acknowledgments

The images in this work are film photographs, shot in 35mm and 120.

Early fragments from this work were previously published in *KNiK* and *Analog Journal*.

My earnest thanks to the friends and family mentioned by name or anonymized in the book. You shape me, you inspire me, and you propel me.

And my heartfelt gratitude to Fred and Edie Ramey for believing in this project from its early days and carrying the torch for its publication with such tenacity. Onward and onward.